SHAKESPEARE'S

TRAGEDY OF CORIOLANUS.

WITH

INTRODUCTION, AND NOTES EXPLANATORY AND CRITICAL

FOR USE IN SCHOOLS AND FAMILIES.

BY THE

REV. HENRY N. HUDSON,

PROFESSOR OF SHAKESPEARE IN BOSTON UNIVERSITY.

———•———

BOSTON, U.S.A.:

PUBLISHED BY GINN & COMPANY.

1899.

TYPOGRAPHY BY J. S. CUSHING & CO., BOSTON, U.S.A.

PRESSWORK BY GINN & CO., BOSTON, U.S.A.

INTRODUCTION.

Date of Composition.

THE TRAGEDY OF CORIOLANUS was never printed till in the folio of 1623, and is among the worst specimens of printing in that volume. The text as there delivered abounds in palpable corruptions : critical sagacity and ingenuity have done their utmost, apparently, towards rectifying the numerous errors, and in not a few cases have been rewarded with fair success ; still there are some passages that seem too much for corrective art.

The tragedy is not heard of at all through any notice or allusion made during the author's life : in fact, we have no contemporary note of reference to it whatever, save in an elegy on Richard Burbage,[1] where we learn that the hero's part was sustained by that celebrated actor. So that we are left without any external evidence as to the date of the writing. Nor does the piece itself contain a traceable vestige of allusion to any known contemporary events ; such, for instance, as that to the new creation of baronets in *Othello*. Our only argument, therefore, as regards the time of composition lies in marks of style, use of language, and complexion of imagery and thought ; in all which respects it clearly falls among the very latest of the Poet's writing. Certainly no

---

[1] Burbage died in 1619, and a copy of an elegy written on that occasion was discovered some years ago among Mr. Heber's manuscripts. See Introduction to *Othello*, page 4.

play of the series surpasses it, and very few, if any, equal it, in boldness of metaphor, in autocratic prerogative of expression, or in passages marked by an overcrowding of matter or an over-compression of language. The strength of civil wisdom, also, the searching anatomy of public characters and motives, the wide and firm grasp of social and political questions, in short, the whole moral and intellectual climate of the piece, — all concur with the former notes in marking it off to the Poet's highest maturity of thought and power. Therewithal I hold it to be among his greatest triumphs in organization : I cannot point out, I believe no one has pointed out, a single instance where the parts might have been better ordered for the proper effect of the whole ; while the interest never once flags or falters, nor suffers any break or diversion, from the beginning to the end : rather say, it holds on with ever-increasing force throughout, and draws all the details into its current ; so that the unity of impression is literally perfect. In this great point of dramatic architecture, I think it bears the palm clean away from both the other Roman tragedies ; and indeed I am not sure but it should be set down as the peer of *Othello*.

Historic Material.

In this, as in the other Roman plays, the historical matter was drawn from Sir Thomas North's translation of Plutarch. The events of the drama as related in the old Greek's *Life of Coriolanus* extend over a period of about four years, from the popular secession to the Sacred Mount, B.C. 494, to the hero's death, B.C. 490. The capture of Corioli is now reckoned to the year B.C. 493.

The severity of criticism applied in recent times has made rather sweeping work with the dim heroic traditions of old

Rome ; insomuch that the story of Coriolanus has now come to be generally regarded as among the most beautiful of the early Roman legends. With these questions, however, Shakespeare of course did not concern himself: like others of his time, he was content to take the rambling and credulous, but lively and graphic narratives of Plutarch as veritable and authentic history. And he would have been every way justifiable in doing this, even if the later arts of historic doubting and sifting, together with the results thereof, had been at his command. For his business as an artist was to set forth a free and life-like portraiture of human character as modified by the old Roman nationality, and clothed with the drapery of the old Roman manners. Here, then, the garrulous and gossiping old story-teller of Cheronea was just the man for him ; since it will hardly be questioned that his tales, whether legendary or not, are replete with the spirit and life of the times and places to which they refer.

The Coriolanus of Plutarch offered the Poet a capital basis for the construction of a great dramatic hero. Hardly any other passage indeed of Roman history could furnish so grand and inviting a theme for personal delineation. The main outlines of the man's character, and also the principal actions ascribed to him, are copied faithfully from the historian ; while those outlines are filled up and finished with a wealth of invention and a depth of judgment which the Poet has perhaps nowhere surpassed. The proportions are indeed gigantic, not to say superhuman ; so much so, that the boldest of delineators might well have scrupled such a portrait, but that he had so strong a warrant of historic faith to bear him out. The other personal figures, also, with the one exception of Menenius Agrippa, were in like sort derived from the same time-honoured repository. And the point most worth noting

is, that from the parts and fragments thence derived, rich and
fresh as these often are, th : Poet should have reproduced, as
it were, the entire form and order of their being, creating an
atmosphere and environing which so fit and cohere with what
he borrowed, that the whole has the air and movement of an
original work.   For it may be observed that all the humorous
and amusing scenes — and Shakespeare has few that are
more choicely conceived or more aptly used — are supplied
from the Poet's own mind ; there being no hint towards these
in Plutarch, except the fable rehearsed and applied by old
Menenius, who is merely described as one of " the pleasantest
old men, and the most acceptable to the people."   And yet
how exquisite the keeping of these scenes with the other
matter of the play ! and how perfectly steeped they seem to
be in the very genius and spirit of the old Roman life and
manners !

Nor does the Poet's borrowing in this case stop with incidents or with lines of character : it extends to the very
words and sentences of the old translator, and this sometimes
for a considerable space together.   In illustration of this, I
copy, with slight abridgment, the passage describing the flight
of Coriolanus to Antium, and his reception by Aufidius :

" It was even twilight when he entered the city, and many
people met him in the streets, but no man knew him.   So
he went immediately to Tullus Aufidius' house, and when he
came thither he got him up straight to the chimney-hearth,
and sat him down, and spake not a word, his face all muffled
over.   They of the house spying him wondered what he
should be, yet they durst not bid him rise : for, disguised as
he was, yet there appeared a certain majesty in his countenance and in his silence ; whereupon they went to Tullus who
was at supper, to tell him of the strange disguising of this

man. Tullus rose presently from the board, and coming towards him asked who he was, and wherefore he came. Then Marcius unmuffled himself, and, after he had paused awhile, said 'If thou knowest me not yet, Tullus, and seeing me dost not believe me to be the man I am indeed, I must of necessity bewray myself to be that I am. I am CAIUS MARCIUS, who hath done to thyself particularly, and to all the Volsces generally, great hurt and mischief, which I cannot deny for my surname CORIOLANUS that I bear. For I never had other benefit of the painful service I have done, and the extreme dangers I have been in, but this surname ; — a good memory and witness of the malice and displeasure thou shouldest bear me. Indeed the name only remaineth with me : for the rest the envy and cruelty of the people of Rome have taken from me, by the sufferance of the dastardly Nobility and magistrates, who have forsaken me, and let me be banished by the people. This extremity hath now driven me to come as a poor suitor, to take thy chimney-hearth : not of any hope I have to save my life thereby ; for if I had feared death, I would not have come hither to put myself in hazard ; but pricked forward with desire to be revenged of them that thus have banished me ; which now I do begin, in putting my person into the hands of their enemies. Wherefore, if thou hast any heart to be wreaked of the injuries thy enemies have done thee, speed thee now, and let my misery serve thy turn, and so use it, that my services may be a benefit to the Volsces ; promising thee that I will fight with better will for you than I did when I was against you ; knowing that they fight more valiantly who know the force of the enemy than such as have never proved it. But if it be so that thou dare not, and art weary to prove fortune any more, then am I also weary to live any longer. And it were no wisdom in thee to save the life of him who hath been here-tofore thy mortal enemy, and whose service now can nothing help nor pleasure thee.' Tullus, hearing what he said, was a marvellous glad man, and, taking him by the hand, said unto him, 'Stand up, O Marcius, and be of good cheer; for in proffering thyself unto us thou doest us great honour; and by this means thou mayest hope also of greater things at all the Volsces' hands.' So he feasted him for that time, and entertained him in the honourablest manner he could, talking with him of no other matter at that present; but within a few days they fell to consultation in what sort they should begin their wars."

To this I must add the still more remarkable passage relating the visit of the Roman ladies to the enemy's camp, and the interview between Volumnia and her son:

" Now was Marcius set in his chair of state, and when he spied the women coming afar off he marvelled what it meant; but afterwards, knowing his wife, who came foremost, he determined at the first to persist in his rancour. But in the end, being altered to see them, his heart would not serve him to tarry their coming to his chair; but, coming down in haste, he went to meet them, and first he kissed his mother and embraced her awhile, then his wife and little children. And nature so wrought in him, that the tears fell from his eyes, and he could not keep himself from making much of them. Then, perceiving that his mother would speak, he called the chiefest of the Volsces to hear what she would say. Then she spake in this sort:

" ' If we held our peace, my son, and determined not to speak, the state of our poor bodies and present sight of our raiment would easily bewray to thee what life we have led at home since thy exile: but think now with thyself how much more unfortunate than all the women living we are come hither, considering that the sight which should be most pleasant to behold, spiteful fortune hath made most fearful to us; making myself to see my son, and my daughter here her husband, besieging the walls of his native country; so as that which is the only comfort to all others in their adversity, to pray unto the gods and to call to them for aid, is the thing which plungeth us in most deep perplexity. For we cannot, alas! together pray both for victory to our country and for safety of thy life; but a world of grievous curses, yea, more than any mortal enemy can heap upon us, are forcibly wrapped up in our prayers. For the bitter sop of most hard choice is offered thy wife and children either to lose the person of thyself or the nurse of their native country. For myself, my son, I am determined not to tarry till fortune in my lifetime do make an end of this war; for, if I cannot persuade thee rather to do good unto both parties than to overthrow and destroy the one, trust unto it, thou shalt no sooner march forward to assault thy country, but thy foot shall tread upon thy mother's womb, that brought thee first into this world. And I may not defer to see the day, either that my son be led prisoner in triumph by his natural countrymen or that he himself do triumph of them. If it were so that my request tended to save thy country in destroying the Volsces, I must confess thou wouldest hardly resolve on that: for, as to destroy thy country is altogether unmeet and unlawful; so were it not just, and less honourable, to betray those that put their trust in thee. But my only demand consisteth to make a jail-delivery of all evils, which delivereth equal benefit and safety to both, but most honourable to the Volsces. For it shall appear that, having victory in their hands, they have granted us singular graces, peace and amity; of which good, if so it come to pass, thyself is the only author, and so hast thou the honour. But, if it fail, thyself alone shall carry the shameful reproach of either party. So, though the end of war be uncertain, yet this is most certain, — that, if it be thy chance to conquer, this benefit shalt thou reap of thy goodly conquest, to be chronicled the plague and destroyer of thy country. And if fortune overthrow thee, then the world will say, that through desire to revenge thy private injuries thou hast for ever undone thy friends who did most lovingly receive thee. — My son, why dost thou not answer me? Dost thou take it honourable for a noble man to remember the wrongs and injuries done him, and dost not think it an honest man's part to be thankful for the goodness that parents do show to their children? No man living is more bound to show himself thankful in all parts and respects than thyself. Thou hast not hitherto showed thy poor mother any courtesy, and therefore it is not only honest, but due unto me, that I should obtain my so just and reasonable request of thee. But since by reason I cannot persuade thee, to what purpose do I defer my last hope?'

"With these words, herself, his wife, and children fell down upon their knees before him. Marcius seeing that could refrain no longer, but went straight and lift her up, crying out, 'O mother, what have you done to me?' And, holding her hard by the right hand, 'O mother,' said he, 'you have won a happy victory for your country, but mortal and unhappy for your son; for I see myself vanquished by you alone.' These words being spoken openly, he spake a little apart with his mother and wife, and then let them return to Rome, for so they did request him; and so, remaining in the camp that night, the next morning he dislodged, and marched into the Volsces' country again."

Shakespeare's Treatment of the Subject.

I have said that Coriolanus as drawn by Plutarch held out strong and taking points of natural aptness for use as a grand dramatic hero, and that the Poet's delineation is marked by a substantial and even formal adherence to the legend in the main outlines of the character. Such a bold structure of old Roman manhood, or, if you please, such a bold reflection of the old Roman ideas and sentiments of manhood, must have been potently fascinating to Shakespeare's mind : it was a subject for him to stretch his powers upon. But the matter, I think, had yet other attractions for him. For the social and political principles involved in those early struggles of the Herculean infant Commonwealth are among the gravest and most fruitful that human history has ever turned up to view. The whole subsequent life and grandeur of the Roman State were depending on the questions then in issue between the several orders of the people. So that the deepest problems of man's social and civil being came along naturally in the train of the hero's character. And Shakespeare's mode of treating the subject shows that he understood all this perfectly. The grand philosophic impartiality with which he weighs the different forces in action, and casts up or carries on in his mind the sum-total of results, fairly argues the matter to have been no less attractive to him as a field for discursive reason than for dramatic representation. The selection and disposing of the incidents, and the whole shaping and drift of the action, are ordered with consummate skill to this end. The historical events are seized not only in their richest poetical aspect, but also in their deepest political relations and bearings. And Shakespeare's mighty intellect may here almost be said to wanton and luxuriate on the very marrow of civil and philosophical discourse; insomuch that we may justly apply in this behalf the saying of Schlegel, that "under the seeming artlessness of adhering closely to history as he found it, a high degree of art is concealed."

Accordingly from the scenes of this play may be gathered, directly or by quick inference, a code and stock of practical wisdom large enough and various enough to furnish out the moralist and the statesman. Especially we here seem to have the concentrated essence of all that has been written, or that can be said, touching the relative claims of aristocracy and democracy. Nor need we travel any further to learn all there is to be known touching the genius and method of demagogic craft and management. In the two Tribunes we have a full-drawn type of the class of men who in every age have made it their business or their pastime to wheedle and cajole and bamboozle the ignorant multitude, and drive them about in herds. At the same time, the rights of the people against those who would insult and oppress them are held in just and steady recognition. The whole work indeed bespeaks a mind which, without any loss of vigour or spirit, has ripened up into a sage-like calmness, clearness, and sobriety; which, as from a world-commanding eminence, has made a full and complete survey of humanity; which knows men through and through, both as individuals and as members of the body politic; and which understands how man and man, rank and rank, class and class, sex and sex, act and react on one another in all the civil and social relations of life: so that he can view and touch them, play or be serious with them, laugh at or instruct them, as one that is thoroughly at home both among and within them. Yet this large and varied science is kept in due subordination to the nature and law of the work, which is in no sort an essay or a treatise, nor carries any shade of a didactic purpose in its face, but is simply an elevation of history into pure drama. If indeed I were to mark the distinctive excellence of the piece, I should set it down as standing in a free union of the moral and political idea with the dramatic, or of the philosophic mind with the poetic.

Rights of the People well Respected.

Hazlitt charges that in this play the Poet shows a strong leaning to the side of Patrician arrogance and pride against the rights and feelings of the people. Therewithal he expatiates at large to make out how much more of poetry there is in the high treadings of aristocratic insolence than in the modest walking of Plebeian humility. According to his notion, a wolf raging among a flock of sheep is a far more poetical object than the terrified flock. This is " an old fond paradox," which would persuade us there is naturally more beauty in the doing of wrong than in the suffering of wrong, thus divorcing poetry from that which is right and good. For my part, I prefer a different faith ; and I confess to finding more of poetry in Burns's " wee, modest crimson-tippèd flower" than in the high-flaunting plant that with its coarse proud face seems to mock the Sun.

There is, I believe, no ground for such a charge as Hazlitt's in this case. On the contrary, the play, I think, may be justly cited as a pattern of dramatic evenhandedness. The ugly and offensive points of the hero, those which draw upon him the people's hatred, are set forth unspar-

ingly; not indeed naked and alone, for this were turning
them into caricature, but in combination with high and
noble traits, just as delivered in the history, and just as we
are finding them perpetually in actual men. So, on the
other side, much that is good and generous in the people,
as well as what is envious and mean, has a kindly and cor-
dial showing, sometimes playful indeed, and sometimes
otherwise; but still so as, in effect, to engage them more of
sympathy than of contempt. They are represented as
bearing much, forgiving much; free to acknowledge the
greatness of the haughty Patrician, and not more resenting
his insolence than regretting it; and never withheld from
making fair returns of honour even against many and great
provocations, till set on fire by the tongues of ambitious
and self-seeking agitators. If there be any person in the
play whom the Poet leans to more than another, it is old
Menenius, a frank, patriotic, liberal soul, who is genially
and lovingly humorous towards the people even when his
eye is upon their faults, yet free and upright in reproving
them, though at the same time mindful of their virtues;
who smilingly stoops to play jokes upon them, that so he
may soothe and sweeten their exasperated minds; using his
good-natured wit to heal as fast as his sharpness wounds;
and thus standing at an equal remove from the insulting
aristocrat and the snaky demagogue.

I will even venture to say that the people as here represented have in them a preponderance of the amiable and
the good, while in the hero there is a clear preponderance
of the reverse. It is true, they are something inconstant
and uncertain in their temper, insomuch as to be reproached
by him that "with every minute they do change a mind";
but he is quite as changeable as they, and withal much less

excusable in his inconstancy. They do not indeed like to be
scorned and mocked by their superiors, especially those who
are soliciting their favour and support; whereas he, in his
overwrought and passionate egotism, takes care to make
them feel his contempt even while he is begging their votes.
To be sure, he is frank and honest in his flouts and scoffs;
but then he might be equally frank and honest in abstaining
from them: or, if he cannot be kind and courteous to the
people without being false to himself, this only argues the
greater viciousness of temper in him. He, in his towering
arrogance, would have his own will stand as an ultimate law
both for himself and for them; but they are far from claim-
ing any such monstrous prerogative over him: it is his pride
to act towards them as if they had no business to exist but
for the pleasure of such as he is; while they are merely
acting on the principle that their own welfare and happiness
should enter into the purpose of their living: he would
stand "as if a man were author of himself, and knew no
other kin," and would have them live entirely for his ends;
whereas they insist on living partly for themselves; and all
they claim is, that he shall own his nature to be kindred
with theirs, and treat them as having the same human heart
which beats in him. Thus their spirit is sociable and sympathetic; his, solitary and exclusive: he craves to dwell
aloft where nothing but his own individuality can breathe;
they prize the life which all have in common, and are for
having the individual will of each tempered into harmony
with that life.

Such is about the aspect which this delineation of old
Roman society wears to me. So regarding it, of course I
cannot see that the hero is glorified at the expense of the
people. He does indeed make a grander figure than they

do : this was required both by the nature of the subject and
by the laws of dramatic interest : but his grandeur, though
it draws the imagination, is of a kind to repel the heart.
We wonder at the man, but are far from loving him or wish-
ing to be like him. True, at the capture of Corioli, the
Poet makes the people fall to plundering, which draws upon
them a storm of reproach from the hero : but this was in
the history ; moreover such has been the practice of common soldiers in all ages and places of the world. In short,
the representation given of the people in this play is at all
points true to the life : so that it does not well appear how
those who despise them as here characterized can fail to
despise them as they are in fact. To my thinking, the
Poet's multitude in this case are both better and wiser than
their Patrician contemner.

Delineation of the Hero.

The remarks already made infer pride to be the backbone
of the hero's character ; this too a pride standing partly
indeed on class and family grounds, but still more on such
as are purely individual or personal. And such is the idea
of the man which Shakespeare found in Plutarch, who pref-
aces his narrative with the following calm and weighty sentences touching the subject :

" While the force and vigour of his soul, and a persevering
constancy in all he undertook, led him successfully into
many noble achievements, yet, on the other side, by indulging the vehemence of his passion, and through an obstinate
reluctance to yield or accommodate his humours and sentiments to those of people about him, he rendered himself
incapable of acting and associating with others. Those who

saw with admiration how proof his nature was against all the softness of pleasure, the hardships of service, and the allurements of gain, while allowing to that universal firmness of his the respective names of temperance, fortitude, and justice, yet, in the life of the citizen and the statesman, could not choose but be disgusted at the severity and ruggedness of his deportment, and with his overbearing, haughty, and imperious temper. Education and study, and the favours of the Muses, confer no greater benefit on those that seek them than these humanizing and civilizing lessons, which teach our natural qualities to submit to the limitations prescribed by reason, and to avoid the wildness of extremes."

In accordance with what is here said, Shakespeare not only makes pride the hero's master-principle, but also sets forth his pride as being rendered altogether inflammable and uncontrollable by passion ; insomuch that, if a spark of provocation is struck into the latter, the former instantly flames up beyond measure, and sweeps away all the regards of prudence, of decorum, and even of common sense. It is therefore strictly characteristic of the man, that an unexpected word of reproach stings him to the quick : the instant it touches his ear, he explodes like a rocket. It is on this that the wily Tribunes work, plying their craft, and watching the time to sting him into some fatal provocation of popular resentment. Hence, also, the Poet, with great judgment, and without any hint from the history, makes Aufidius, when the time is ripe for firing off the conspiracy against his life, touch him into an ecstasy of passionate rage by spitting the term *boy* at him. Now his very pride, if duly guarded by the strengths of reason and self-respect, would have caused him, from the utter unfitness of such an epithet, to answer it with calm and silent scorn : but he re-

sents it in proportion as it strikes wide of him, and makes its
very absurdity the cause of its power over him.

The people, too, would gladly reward his noble acts with
the highest honours in their gift, but that, to their sense, " he
pays himself with being proud." They glory in his valour
and prowess ; his strength of heart and of hand is to them a
theme of willing praise ; but they complain, as they well may,
that he is too proud of being so valiant : nay, an instinct of
social reason tells them, and truly too, that his heroic exploits
are done rather with a view to nurse and pamper his pride
and self-will than from any impulse of patriotism, of public
spirit, or even of honourable ambition : in short, it is not at
all to win their respect and goodwill, but only to feed his in-
ordinate egotism, that he enacts the hero. They are even
so liberal as to grant that the fault is something ingenerate
in his nature, so that he cannot altogether help it, and are
ready to make large allowance for him on this score : but
then the more he helps them by his deeds, the more he
wounds them with his insolence ; nay, he seems to delight
in serving them, only that he may turn his service into a
vantage-ground for spurning them ; and this is what they
cannot bear, because it seems to them, as indeed it is, truly
inhuman, and renders him unfit for any sort of intercourse
with men.

There is withal much in the people that is really not deserving of respect. This the hero seizes on greedily, and
makes the most of, as favouring that whereon his pride
mainly fastens ; and at the same time winks away whatever
there is in them of redeeming quality : he scorns their mean-
ness, and is glad to find it in them, as giving him cause for
scorning them : he prefers to see in them nothing but what
is vile, and would fain make them as vile as he thinks them

to be, that so his contempt may stand justified in his own sight. Still he is placed where his pride cannot reach its mark but by their suffrage; for its dearest gratification, he must pay his court to that which most galls and offends it. Here the people have a strong hold upon him. So nothing will do but that he try to extort their admiration and suffrage while making them hate his person: what he most prides himself upon is to have his greatness force honours from them notwithstanding his insolence to them; because such a contradiction between their feeling and their voting serves to emphasize his superiority. This is well shown in what falls from one of those almost characterless speakers in whom the Poet sometimes puts much candour and shrewdness of observation, and then uses them as the mouthpiece of his own judgment: "If he did not care whether he had their love or no, he'd waved indifferently 'twixt doing them neither good nor harm; but he seeks their hate with greater devotion than they can render it him, and leaves nothing undone that may fully discover him their opposite." Hence, when he goes out to beg their voices, he is careful to spice his requests with mockery, and to let them see that his spirit disclaims what his tongue speaks: then, if they excuse his spirit on the score of his formal compliance, this will be his triumph, and his pride will take a special benefit in their pocketing of his insults.

It is a bold but most natural stroke of character, that the hero, notwithstanding his alleged intense aversion to seeming at all the thing he is not, can yet dissemble to perfection when the doing so does not conflict with his ruling passion. From his bearing towards the people, one would suppose it were quite impossible for him to practise any sort of counterfeit or concealment. On this ground Menenius apologizes for his rough bluntness of manner:

His nature is too noble for the world:
He would not flatter Neptune for his trident,
Or Jove for's power to thunder.   His heart's his mouth:
What his breast forges, that his tongue must vent.

Consider this: He has been bred i' the wars
Since he could draw a sword, and is ill school'd
In bolted language; meal and bran together
He throws without distinction.

Thus others think him, and he thinks himself, utterly incapable of simulating any thing on the outside that is not really in his heart.   And, when his friends entreat him to comply externally and in form with the people's humour, it really seems a necessity of nature with him to be the same without as he is within: so, after trying his best, apparently, to frame his mind to their request, he frankly declares at last,

I will not do't;
Lest I surcease to honour mine own truth,
And by my body's action teach my mind
A most inherent baseness.

But all this, as the sequel proves, is simply because his pride does not draw in that direction, or rather draws directly the other way.   For, after the sentence of exile, and when he is preparing to leave, he forthwith goes to practising the closest reserve and concealment of his mind, and appears indeed a complete master in dissimulative art.   With his inner man in a perfect tempest of passion, he is nevertheless outwardly calm and serene: while the darkest thoughts of revenge are boiling within, his face and speech carry the style of the blandest and smoothest composure.   And he not only seems placid and quiet himself, while his mother is deeply agitated with grief and anger, but goes to schooling her with her own former lessons of calmness and patience, reminding her how she " used to load him with precepts that would make invincible the heart that conn'd them " ; insomuch that none suspect the stormy resolves and purposes he is forming. In all which his action is no doubt spontaneous, and proceeds rather from an instinct of passion than from any conscious art : but this only infers the more strongly how the same cause which, before, prevented his dissembling, now renders him a consummate dissembler. As he was then too proud to be other in mouth than he was in heart towards the people, so here his pride naturally puts him upon making his face the visard and not the index of his mind. Egotism and conscience are indeed very different things. But they sometimes get strangely mixed.

Coriolanus, however, is not altogether " himself his world and his own god " : his will no doubt is to be so, and this is perhaps the most constant force in him ; but he has other and better forces, which often rise against his egotism, and sometimes prevail over it, and at last carry the victory clean away from it. His character indeed is not a little mixed : and all its parts, good and bad, are fashioned on so large a scale as to yield matter enough for making out a strong case either way, according as the observer's mind is set to a course of all blame or all praise ; while at the same time the several lines are so bold and pronounced, that it is not easy for one to keep clear of all extremes, and so to take the impression of a given side as to fit the subject all round. Nor is his pride, with all its anti-social harshness, destitute of amiable and engaging features. There are some points of nobleness and magnanimity about it : the various regards of rank, family, country, talents, and courage enter into its composition, causing it to partake the general greatness of his character ; and as it grows partly by what he derives from and

shares with others, as well as by what is peculiar to himself,
so it involves much of the spirit that commonly issues in
great virtues as well as great faults.   Hence it is not such as,
of itself, to burn out the better juices of manhood : modesty, gratitude, openness of heart and hand, go in company
with it.   And so far it is of a genius and temper to keep
clean and sweet the breast where it dwells ; the principle of
that inward discipline under which tenderness of heart, purity
and rectitude of life, and many of the milder and gentler
qualities have their best cherishing ; a natural source of re-
plenishment to whatever virtues it guards, because its own
best nourishment is in the noble growth it fosters.   Which is
well evinced in that, with all his passionate craving of renown, he still counts it among his chief honours to be the
cause that others are honoured.   And if he is jealous of
the position of his fellow Patricians, he is jealous of their
merit too ; would guard their virtue as carefully as their
rank ; is not less strenuous to have them deserve than to
have them hold the place of supreme power and reverence
in the State.   So the Poet read in Plutarch how he besought
the Patricians "to let the people know by their deeds, that
they did not so much pass them in power and riches as in
true nobility and valiantness."   Nor should it be omitted
that the admission of the people to a direct share in the
government is a new thing with them : he is not used to it ;
he resents it as an invasion of ancient right ; he fears it as
a seed of political anarchy and dissolution.   Old Rome was
indeed a wonderful nation : Shakespeare could not but be
fascinated with the record of its splendours and greatness ;
and the hero's character offered him an apt and inviting
occasion for representing the struggle between those two
antagonist forces in the State whose reconcilement and unity

did so much towards building and cementing the mighty structure.

I have spoken of the hero's modesty; yet I have to confess that there is something rather equivocal about it. He cannot indeed frame his mouth to the language of flattery, and he has an honest aversion to being flattered; and so far his temper is noble and just. Withal it seems really to offend him to hear himself praised; yet he is so ostentatious and emphatic, not to say supercilious, in his disgust of the thing, as to breed some doubt whether, after all, it is any thing but egotism in disguise, or whether it is not rather the offspring of arrogance than of real modesty. When he so energetically scouts to " hear his nothings monster'd," there is in his manner a strong relish of haughty contempt for his praisers, or a certain censorious loftiness of mind, as if he craved occasions for rebuking his friends and admirers, and of making them feel his immense superiority. Men have sometimes towered so high in self-approval as to scorn the approval of their fellow-men. And so our hero's behaviour in this point smacks a good deal as if his self-applause were so enormous, that the strongest applause of others seems to him utterly inadequate, or as if he felt his greatness to be of so transcendent a pitch as to " make breath poor and speech unable." Such a desperate calenture of egotism may, and sometimes does, pass for modesty, for it is apt to use the style of that virtue; the man seeming to shrink from the voice of praise, while in truth his extreme self-sufficiency merely leads him to think that none are able to appreciate him, or good enough to praise him. That Shakespeare saw the germs of this disease in the deep intricacies of the human heart, is apparent from his saying of another famous character, that " he speaks not to himself but with a pride that

quarrels at self-breath." And the delineation of Coriolanus
has many notes which infer the man's disdaining of honours
to be at least partly in the idea that no honours can come up
to his merit. That the Poet conceived this as among the
hero's traits of character, becomes evident when he makes
his arrogance reach the height of supposing that all Rome
cannot counterpoise his own gigantic importance. On being
banished, Coriolanus assumes that the loss of his single person will be worse for Rome than the loss of Rome will be
to him ; and so retorts the sentence with —

> You common cry of curs ! whose breath I hate
> As reek o' the rotten fens, whose loves I prize
> As the dead carcasses of unburied men
> That do corrupt my air, — *I banish you.*

The Hero and his Mother.

But the man, it must be confessed, is gloriously proud of
his mother : in fact, his pride in her is only less than his
pride of personal greatness and of self. This is the one
point indeed where his pride relaxes its anti-social stiffness,
and ceases to be individual and exclusive. And it is very
considerable that he appears noblest and strongest just when
his nature outwrestles his purpose, and when his pride
breaks down under the weight of filial reverence and duty.
Shakespeare had it before him in Plutarch, that "the only
thing which caused him to love honour was the delight his
mother had of him ; for nothing made him so happy as that
she might always see him return with a crown upon his
head, and still embrace him, with tears running down her
cheeks for joy." And so, as represented in the drama, he
can outface the rest of the world, but his mother, with his
household treasures at her side, is too much for him : when

he has conquered all the armies of his country, and has the State itself at his feet, her eloquence, her strength of soul, and patriotic devotion conquer him. In his rapture of self-will, he aspires to act the god, and thinks to stifle the heart's instincts, and to rise above the natural emotions; and he stands most redeemed to our judgment and our sense of manliness, when at last a diviner power than will masters him, and the sacred regards of home triumph over his self-sufficiency, and his arrogance succumbs to the touch of domestic awe and tenderness, and he frankly yields himself human. Where have we another such an instance of pride struggling with affection, and of an iron will subdued by the spontaneous forces of the human breast, as when he sees the embassy of women approaching?

> My wife comes foremost; then the honour'd mould
> Wherein this trunk was framed, and in her hand
> The grandchild to her blood. — But out, affection!
> All bond and privilege of nature, break!
> Let it be virtuous to be obstinate. —
> What is that curtsy worth? or those doves' eyes,
> Which can make gods forsworn? I melt, and am not
> Of stronger earth than others. My mother bows;
> As if Olympus to a molehill should
> In supplication nod; and my young boy
> Hath an aspéct of intercession, which
> Great Nature cries *Deny not*.

I know not where to look for a grander picture than we have in the same scene afterwards, when the conqueror's haughtiness and parricidal hardness gradually limber and soften, and at length fall clean away, at the voice of mater-nal intercession. Such a mingling of austerity and tender-ness is met with nowhere else in Shakespeare's poetry. And it is to be noted that the mother's triumph does not seem to be fully consummated, till her great woman's heart stiffens up with something of the son's pride, and she turns away with an air of defiance :

> Come, let us go :
> This fellow had a Volscian to his mother;
> His wife is in Corioli, and this child
> Like him by chance.

That she can be like him in pride thaws down that temper somewhat in him, and disposes him to be like her in other points. In accordance with his usual method, the Poet prepares us for this crowning victory of the mother by a lighter example in the same kind. I refer to the scene, iii. 2, where Volumnia urges her son to appease the infuriated multitude by playing the amiable towards them. His pride snaps off an intense repugnance to the undertaking, and she subdues him to it :

> At thy choice, then :
> To beg of thee, it is my more dishonour
> Than thou of them.   Come all to ruin : let
> Thy mother rather feel thy pride than fear
> Thy dangerous stoutness; for I mock at death
> With as big heart as thou.   Do as thou list.
> Thy valiantness was mine, thou suck'dst it from me;
> But own'st thy pride thyself.

The Hero and his Wife.

Nor is the mother's the only influence at work to break the hero out of his unnatural purpose and recall him to better thoughts. She indeed does nearly all the speaking ; but her speech is powerfully reinforced by the presence and aspect of others. Little is said of Virgilia, and still less is said by her ; but that little is so managed as to infer a great deal. A very gentle, retiring, undemonstrative person, she has withal much quiet firmness, and even a dash of something very like obstinacy, in her disposition. Her power touches the centre of her husband's heart; and it does this the better for being the power of delicacy and sweetness; a power the more effective with him, that it is so utterly unlike his own. So, when he returns from the war all covered with glory, her silent tears of joy are to him a sweeter tribute than the loud applause of all the rest: he hails her as "my gracious silence," and plays out his earnest tenderness in the question, "Wouldst thou have laugh'd had I come coffin'd home, that weep'st to see me triumph?" How deeply her still forces have stolen into his being, is charmingly evinced in what he says to her when she comes with her speechless supplication to second the voice of maternal remonstrance:

> Best of my flesh,
> Forgive my tyranny; but do not say
> For that, *Forgive our Romans.* O, a kiss
> Long as my exile, sweet as my revenge!
> Now, by the jealous Queen of Heaven, that kiss
> I carried from thee, dear, and my true lip
> Hath virgin'd it e'er since.

Here he finds his entire household in something more powerful than arms to resist him; the mother, the wife, the child, all are shaming his parricidal revenge by standing true to their fatherland against the son, the husband, and the father; and the words just quoted show that the might of the silent mourner is even more penetrating than that of the eloquent pleader. The two women have hearts stronger in love than his in pride; and the prime object of that love is the old Rome of their fathers: both the mother and the wife are steadfastly resolved that, if he march any further against that object, it shall be over their bodies; while the boy's Roman spirit flashes up in the strange declaration, "'A shall

not tread on me ; I'll run away till I am bigger, then I'll
fight." The hideous unnaturalness of his course is brought
fully home to him at thus seeing that the very childhood of
his own flesh and blood is instinctively bent on resisting him,
and will sooner disown his kindred and make war upon
him than give way to his fury against their common nurse.
Therewithal, in the presence of "the noble sister of Publicola, the Moon of Rome," he sees how all that is most illus-
trious in the same proud Patrician stock on which he so
much prides himself, even those who were most hurt in his
banishment, will rather unite with his banishers in imploring
the gods against him than surrender their country to his
revenge. And I am apt to think that what most took
Shakespeare in this ancient tale of Roman patriotism was,
that while, to the minds of those high-souled men and
women, it was a great thing to be Patricians, to be Romans
was a much greater.

Roman Womanhood.

A nation's favourite legends have a very close connection
with its character, and are indeed the spontaneous out-
growth of its peculiar genius and spirit : that they reflect its
ideals of right and good is what gives them life and cur-
rency. Now, in the primitive Roman scheme of thought,
the warrior held the first place, the mother the second.
Womanhood in general was indeed a great power in old
Rome, and to be a mother was the highest honour but one.
Veneration of the matronage was the delight and pride of
early Roman manhood : the gods were believed on several
occasions to have bestowed special blessings and deliver-
ances on the commonwealth through the women : temples

were built, high honours paid to womanhood, in the faith that the women had repeatedly been the salvation of their country from ruin; and in the intercession which prevailed with our hero the women were held to have been kindled and moved to the undertaking by the special inspiration of the gods. In short, the men of old Rome seem to have thought that the gods would forthwith abandon them, if they ceased to respect their mothers and their wives.

In the legend of Coriolanus the hero's character stands out as a special impersonation of the two great ideas of martial courage and prowess, and of filial piety and submission. From this point, it draws deep into the general system of Roman morals and manners. Reverence for parents, the religion of home, the sacredness of the domestic enclosure, worship of the household gods, whatever shed consecration on the family, and surrounded it with the angels of piety and awe, — these were the corner-stone of the old Roman discipline, the palladium of the national strength and virtue. To fight bravely, to suffer heroically, for their country, were the outposts of manhood, the outside and public parts of manly honour; while its heart and centre stood in having something at home worth fighting and suffering for: of this something motherhood was the soul; and their best thoughts drew to the point of being "more brave for this, that they had much to love."

Character of Volumnia.

In this view, Volumnia aptly impersonates the woman's and the mother's side of the Roman system. She is a superb figure indeed, yet a genuine woman throughout, though with a high strain of what may be called manliness pervading her womanhood. She has all of her son's essential strength and greatness of character, and is nearly as proud withal as he : but her pride has a much less individual and unsocial cast ; he is the chief matter of her pride, while self is the chief matter of his : she is proud of him too far more for her country's sake than either for his or her own : her supreme ambition is that he should be the greatest among the Romans ; and she would have his greatness stand in being more a Roman than any of the others. Hence her pride flames out in fierce resentment at the sentence of exile : her maternal heart boils over with passion, insomuch that to those who are nowise in sympathy with her anger she seems insane ; and she bangs away at the Tribunes with the wildest notes of imprecation :

> I would the gods had nothing else to do
> But to confirm my curses ! Could I meet 'em
> But once a-day, it would unclog my heart
> Of what lies heavy to't ;

then hotly remonstrates against the quiet weeping grief of her daughter-in-law :

> Anger's my meat ; I sup upon myself,
> And so shall starve with feeding. — Come, let's go :
> Leave this faint puling, and lament as I do,
> In anger, Juno-like.

Against the people also she goes into a lingual tempest, and speaks as if she would gladly see Rome burnt, since Rome rejects her heart's idol ; but the sequel shows this to be all because she is so intensely Roman in spirit : when things come to the pinch, her actions speak quite another language ; and she is as far from sympathizing with her son in his selfish vindictiveness as she had been from sympathiz-

ing with the people's madness in banishing him. That a
Roman should fight his way to the highest honours in Rome,
is just what she believes in; but that he should fight for any
thing but Rome, is beyond her conception. So, when she
sees her son waging war against his country, where his home
and all its treasures are, she considers him to have renounced
the only cause for fighting at all. It seems to her that he is
making war against the one sole object or end of war; and
she will rather disclaim her part in him than take part with
him; nay, will rather die with Rome than see him grow by
the death of that for which alone, in her view, a Roman
should wish to live.

As the mother's pride is tempered by a more disinterested
and patriotic spirit than the son's, so she holds a much more
firm and steady course: her words, in moments of high resentment, fly about wildly indeed, but her heart sticks fast
to its cherished aims. And her energy of thought and purpose, if not greater than her son's, yet in the end triumphs
over his, because it proceeds on grounds less selfish and personal. She knows and feels that the gods are with her in
it. The Poet wisely, and out of his own invention, repre-
sents her as exhorting him to temporize with the people, and
to use arts for conciliating them which have no allowance in
his bosom's truth:

> I pr'ythee now, my son,
> Go to them, with this bonnet in thy hand;
> And—thus far having stretch'd it, (here be with them,)
> Thy knee bussing the stones, waving thy head,
> Which often, thus, correcting thy stout heart,
> Bow, humble as the ripest mulberry
> That will not hold the handling—say to them,
> Thou art their soldier, and, being bred in broils,
> Hast not the soft way which, thou dost confess,
> Were fit for thee to use, as they to claim,

In asking their good loves; but thou wilt frame
Thyself, forsooth, hereafter theirs, so far
As thou hast power and person.

For even so, like a true woman, as she is, she "would dis-semble with her nature, where her fortune and her friends at stake required she should do so in honour." To her sense and judgment of things, deeds are to be weighed more by their ends and effects in regard of others than by their intrinsic quality to the doer's mind; that is, a man should act rather with a view to help and gladden and comfort those about him, to serve his country and his kind, than to feed his moral egotism, or any sullen pride or humour of self-applause. It is even a rule of honour with her, that a man should, in his action, be more considerate of what will further the welfare and happiness of others than of what will please himself, or accord with any inward or ideal standard of his own. And so it is rightly in woman's nature, as being less wilful and more sympathetic in her reason, to judge of actions mainly by the practical consequences which she hopes or fears therefrom; I mean the consequences not only or chiefly to herself, but to those whom she loves. Therefore it is that women have so often been peace-makers in men's wars of opinions and passions and ideas; and I know not what would become of human society if their softer bosom did not come in to mitigate the sharpness of the brain.

Volumnia, though something more admirable than lovely in her style, is a capital representative of the old Roman matronly character, in which strength and dignity seem to have had rather the better of sweetness and delicacy, but which enshrined the very soul of rectitude and honour. And what a story does the life of this mother and this son, with their reciprocal action and influence, as set forth in the play, tell us of the old Roman domestic system, and of the religious awe of motherhood which formed so large and powerful an element in the social constitution of that wonderful people ! What a comment, too, does all this, taken together with the history of that nation, read upon the Divine precept, "Honour thy father and thy mother, that thy days may be long in the land which the Lord thy God giveth thee" ! For reverence of children to their parents is the principle that binds together successive generations in one continuous life. It is only by men's thinking and acting as in "the presence of canonized forefathers," that the elements of disorder in human nature can be withheld from running to fatal extremes. So that the loosening or impairing of this tie may well be feared as the beginning of domestic and social dissolution ; since they who forget or disown their fathers and mothers will naturally be forgotten and disowned in turn by their children ; if indeed the very soul of parental instinct and religion does not get stifled out of them under a stress of luxury and selfishness. For the decay of filial respect and piety has sometimes gone so far, that men and women have come to regard it as among the greatest of evils to be fathers and mothers.

The Volscian Chief.

Tullus Aufidius makes a very effective foil to Coriolanus, the contrast between them being pressed forward in just the right way to show off the vein of true nobleness which there is in the latter. He has all the pride and passionateness of the hero, without any of his gratitude and magnanimity. In Coriolanus the spirit of rivalry and emulation never passes the bounds of honour ; in the other, it turns to downright personal envy and hate. The hero glories in him as an antagonist, and loves to whip him in fair fight, but is far above all thought of ruining him or stabbing him in the dark. The shocking speech of Aufidius, in the first scene where he appears after the taking of Corioli, is a skilful forecast and premonition of his transport of baseness at the close :

> Nor sleep nor sanctuary,
> Being naked, sick; nor fane nor Capitol,
> The prayers of priests nor times of sacrifice,
> Embankments all of fury, shall lift up
> Their rotten privilege and custom 'gainst
> My hate to Marcius : where I find him, were it
> At home, upon my brother's guard, even there,
> Against the hospitable canon, would I
> Wash my fierce hand in's heart.

Hereupon Coleridge comments as follows : "I have such deep faith in Shakespeare's heart-lore, that I take for granted that this is in nature ; although I cannot in myself discover any germ of possible feeling, which could wax and unfold itself into such a sentiment." The speech is hard indeed ; but I do not take it as a fair index of the speaker's real mind : it seems to me but one of those violent ebullitions of rage in which men's hearts are not so bad as their tongues ; the impulsive extravagance of a very ambitious and inconstant nature writhing in an agony of disappointment. In such cases, dark thoughts often bubble up from unseen depths in the mind, yet do not crystallize into character. Still it must be owned that Aufidius comes pretty near putting the thought of the speech into act at last. Verplanck has a happy comment on the passage : "The mortification of defeat embitters Aufidius' rivalry into hatred. When, afterwards, his banished rival appeals to his nobler nature, that hatred dies away, and his generous feeling revives. Bitter jealousy and hatred again grow up, as his glories are eclipsed by his former adversary; yet this dark passion, too, finally yields to a generous sorrow at his rival's death. I think I have observed very similar alternations of such mixed motives and sentiments, in eminent men, in the collisions of political life."

CORIOLANUS.

PERSONS REPRESENTED.

CAIUS MARCIUS CORIOLANUS.
YOUNG MARCIUS, his Son.
MENENIUS AGRIPPA, his Friend.
TITUS LARTIUS,) Generals against
COMINIUS,   ) the Volscians.
SICINIUS VELUTUS,) Tribunes of the
JUNIUS BRUTUS,   ) People.
A Roman Herald.
TULLUS AUFIDIUS, General of the Volscians.

Lieutenant to Aufidius.
Conspirators with Aufidius.
A Citizen of Antium.
Two Volscian Guards.

VOLUMNIA, Mother to Coriolanus.
VIRGILIA, Wife to Coriolanus.
VALERIA, Friend to Virgilia.
Gentlewoman attending Virgilia.

Roman and Volscian Senators, Patricians, Ædiles, Lictors, Soldiers, Citizens, Messengers, Servants to Aufidius, and other Attendants.

SCENE.—*Partly in Rome and its neighbourhood; partly in the Territories of the Volscians and Antiates.*

ACT I.

SCENE I. — *Rome. A Street.*

Enter a Company of mutinous Citizens, with staves, clubs, and other weapons.

1 Cit. Before we proceed any further, hear me speak.

Citizens. Speak, speak.

1 Cit. You are all resolved rather to die than to famish?

Citizens. Resolved, resolved.

1 Cit. First, you know Caius Marcius is chief enemy to the people.

Citizens. We know't, we know't.

1 Cit. Let us kill him, and we'll have corn at our own price. Is't a verdict?

Citizens. No more talking on't; let it be done: away, away!

2 Cit. One word, good citizens.

1 Cit. We are accounted poor citizens; the patricians, good.[1] What authority surfeits on would relieve us: if they would yield us but the superfluity, while it were wholesome, we might guess they relieved us humanely; but they think we are too dear: the leanness that afflicts us, the object of our misery,[2] is as an inventory to particularize their abundance; our sufferance is a gain to them. Let us revenge this with our pikes, ere we become rakes:[3] for the gods know I speak this in hunger for bread, not in thirst for revenge.

2 Cit. Would you proceed especially against Caius Marcius?

1 Cit. Against him first: he's a very dog to the commonalty.

2 Cit. Consider you what services he has done for his country?

1 Cit. Very well; and could be content to give him good report for't, but that he pays himself with being proud.

2 Cit. Nay, but speak not maliciously.

---

1 *Good* seems to be here used in a double sense, one of them being the commercial; as by Shylock in *The Merchant of Venice:* "My meaning, in saying he is a *good* man, is to have you understand me, that he is sufficient."

2 Meaning, apparently, the *sight* or *spectacle* of their misery; their *leanness* was the *object* that served, by comparison, to remind the Patricians of their own abundance; and so the sufferings of the Plebs were a gain to them.

3 "As lean as a *rake*" was an ancient proverb; *rake* being from *rache*, which signifies a *greyhound*. *Pike* or *pikefork* is also an old word for *pitchfork*. Of course a quibble is intended on *rake*.

1 Cit. I say unto you, what he hath done famously, he did it to that end: though soft-conscienced men can be content to say it was for his country, he did it to please his mother, and partly to be proud; which he is, even to the altitude of his virtue.

2 Cit. What he cannot help in his nature, you account a vice in him. You must in no way say he is covetous.

1 Cit. If I must not, I need not be barren of accusations; he hath faults, with surplus, to tire in repetition. [*Shouts within.*] What shouts are these? The other side o' the city is risen: why stay we prating here? to the Capitol!

Citizens. Come, come.

1 Cit. Soft! who comes here?

2 Cit. Worthy Menenius Agrippa; one that hath always loved the people.

1 Cit. He's one honest enough: would all the rest were so!

Enter MENENIUS AGRIPPA.

Men. What work's, my countrymen, in hand? where go you
With bats and clubs? the matter? speak, I pray you.

1 Cit. Our business is not unknown to the Senate; they have had inkling, this fortnight, what we intend to do, which now we'll show em in deeds. They say poor suitors have strong breaths: they shall know we have strong arms too.

Men. Why, masters, my good friends, mine honest neighbours,
Will you undo yourselves?

1 Cit. We cannot, sir, we are undone already.

Men. I tell you, friends, most charitable care
Have the patricians of you. For your wants,

Your suffering in this dearth, you may as well
Strike at the heaven with your staves as lift them
Against the Roman State; whose course will on
The way it takes, cracking ten thousand curbs
Of more strong link asunder than can ever
Appear in your impediment: for the dearth,
The gods, not the patricians, make it; and
Your knees to them, not arms, must help. Alack,
You are transported by calamity
Thither where more attends you; and you slander
The helms[4] o' the State, who care for you like fathers,
When you curse them as enemies.

1 Cit. Care for us! True, indeed, they ne'er cared for
us yet; suffer us to famish, and their store-houses cramm'd
with grain; make edicts for usury, to support usurers; repeal daily any wholesome Act established against the rich;
and provide more piercing statutes daily, to chain up and
restrain the poor. If the wars eat us not up, they will; and
there's all the love they bear us.

Men. Either you must
Confess yourselves wondrous malicious,
Or be accused of folly. I shall tell you
A pretty tale: it may be you have heard it;
But, since it serves my purpose, I will venture
To stale't[5] a little more.

1 Cit. Well, I'll hear it, sir: yet you must not think to

---

[4] *Helms* for *helmsmen;* as we have *fife* for *fifer, trumpet* for *trumpeter,*
&c.

[5] *Make* it stale, common, or familiar. The Poet often uses *stale* thus, as
in the well-known passage in *Antony and Cleopatra:* "Age cannot wither
her, nor custom *stale* her infinite variety." And in *Julius Cæsar:* "Were I
a common laugher, or did use to *stale* with ordinary oaths my love."

fob-off[6] our disgrace with a tale: but, an't please you, deliver.

Men. There was a time when all the body's members
Rebell'd against the belly; thus accused it:
That only like a gulf it did remain
I' the midst o' the body, idle and unactive,
Still cupboarding the viand, never bearing
Like labour with the rest; where[7] th' other instruments
Did see and hear, devise, instruct, walk, feel,
And, mutually participant, did minister
Unto the appetite and affection common
Of the whole body. The belly answer'd, —

1 Cit. Well, sir,
What answer made the belly?

Men. Sir, I shall tell you. With a kind of smile,
Which ne'er came from the lungs, but even thus —
For, look you, I may make the belly smile
As well as speak — it tauntingly replied
To th' discontented members, the mutinous parts
That envied his receipt; even so most fitly
As you malign our Senators for that
They are not such as you.

1 Cit. Your belly's answer? What!
The kingly-crownèd head, the vigilant eye,
The counsellor heart, the arm our soldier,
Our steed the leg, the tongue our trumpeter,

---

[6] Mrs. Quickly, in speaking of Falstaff's debt to her, 2 *King Henry IV.*,
ii. 1, uses this phrase in a little different form: "I have borne, and borne,
and borne, and been *fubb'd off*, and fubb'd off, and fubb'd off, from this day
to that, that it is a shame to be thought on."

[7] In the Poet's time, *where* was often used for *whereas;* also, *whereas*
for *where.*

With other muniments and petty helps
In this our fabric, if that they —
    Men.   What then? —
'Fore me, this fellow speaks! — what then? what then?
    1 Cit. — Should by the cormorant belly be restrain'd,
Who is the sink o' the body, —
    Men.   Well, what then?
    1 Cit. — The former agents, if they did complain,
What could the belly answer?
    Men.   I will tell you;
If you'll bestow a small — of what you've little —
Patience awhile, you'll hear the belly's answer.
    1 Cit. Ye're long about it.
    Men.   Note me this, good friend;
Your most grave belly was deliberate,
Not rash like his accusers, and thus answer'd:
True is it, my incorporate friends, quoth he,
That I receive the general food at first,
Which you do live upon; and fit it is,
Because I am the store-house and the shop
Of the whole body: but, if you do remember,
I send it through the rivers of your blood,
Even to the Court, the heart, to th' seat o' the brain;[8]
And, through the cranks and offices[9] *of man,*
The strongest nerves and small inferior veins

---

[8] According to the old philosophy, the heart was the seat of the understanding; hence it is here called "the Court." So in a previous speech: "The counsellor heart."

[9] *Cranks* are *windings;* the meandering ducts of the human body. — *Offices* was used for *rooms* or *apartments*, and such is its meaning here. — The words *nerve, vein, artery,* and *sinew* are used very loosely, almost indiscriminately indeed, by Shakespeare: in fact they had not then got differentiated to their present use.

From me receive that natural competency
Whereby they live : and though that all at once,
You, my good friends, — this says the belly, mark me, —

   1 Cit. Ay, sir ; well, well.

   Men.   *Though all at once cannot*
See what I do deliver out to each,
Yet I can make my audit up, that all
From me do back receive the flour of all,
And leave me but the bran.   What say you to't? [10]

   1 Cit. It was an answer : how apply you this?

   Men. The Senators of Rome are this good belly,
And you the mutinous members : for, examine
Their counsels and their cares ; digest things rightly
Touching the weal o' the common ; you shall find,
No public benefit which you receive
But it proceeds or comes from them to you,
And no way from yourselves. — What do you think,
You, the great toe of this assembly?

   1 Cit. I the great toe ! why the great toe?

   Men. For that, being one o' the lowest, basest, poorest,
Of this most wise rebellion, thou go'st foremost :
Thou rascal, that art worst in blood to run, [11]

---

[10] The fable of *The Belly and the Members* has been traced far back in antiquity. It is found in several ancient collections of Æsopian fables ; so that there is as much reason for making Æsop the author of this as of many others that go in his name. Shakespeare was acquainted with a very spirited version of it in Camden's *Remains ;* but he was chiefly indebted for the matter to North's Plutarch.

[11] *Rascal* and *in blood* are terms of the forest, both here used equivocally. The meaning seems to be, " thou worthless scoundrel, though thou art in the worst plight for running of all this herd of plebeians, like a deer not *in blood,* thou takest the lead in this tumult in order to obtain some private advantage to thyself." " Worst n blood " has a secondary meaning of *lowest in condition.*

Lead'st first to win some vantage. —
But make you ready your stiff bats and clubs:
Rome and her rats are at the point of battle;
The one side must have bale.[12] —

Enter CAIUS MARCIUS.

Hail, noble Marcius!

Mar. Thanks. — What's the matter, you dissentious rogues,
That, rubbing the poor itch of your opinion,
Make yourselves scabs?

1 Cit. We have ever your good word.

Mar. He that will give good words to ye will flatter
Beneath abhorring. What would you have, you curs,
That like nor peace nor war? the one affrights you,
The other makes you proud. He that trusts to you,
Where he should find you lions, finds you hares;
Where foxes, geese: you are no surer, no,
Than is the coal of fire upon the ice,
Or hailstone in the sun. Your virtue is,
To make him worthy whose offence subdues him,
And curse that justice did it.[13] Who deserves greatness
Deserves your hate; and your affections are
A sick man's appetite, who desires most that
Which would increase his evil. He that depends
Upon your favours swims with fins of lead,
And hews down oaks with rushes. Trust ye? Hang ye!
With every minute you do change your mind;
And call him noble that was now your hate,

---

12 *Bale* is *evil* or *mischief*. The word is pure Saxon, and was becoming obsolete in Shakespeare's time.

13 " Your virtue is to speak well of him whom his own offences have subjected to justice; and to rail at those laws by which he was punished."

Him vile that was your garland.   What's the matter,
That in these several places of the city
You cry against the noble Senate, who,
Under the gods, keep you in awe, which else
Would feed on one another? — What's their seeking?

   Men.   For corn at their own rates; whereof, they say,
The city is well stored.

   Mar.   Hang 'em!   They say!
They'll sit by th' fire,[14] and presume to know
What's done i' the Capitol; who's like to rise,
Who thrives, and who declines; side factions, and give out
Conjectural marriages; making parties strong,
And feebling such as stand not in their liking
Below their cobbled shoes.   They say there's grain enough!
Would the nobility lay aside their ruth,[15]
And let me use my sword, I'd make a quarry [16]
With thousands of these quarter'd slaves, as high
As I could pick [17] my lance.

   Men.   Nay, these are almost thoroughly persuaded;
For though abundantly they lack discretion,
Yet are they passing cowardly.   But, I beseech you,
What says the other troop?

   Mar.   They are dissolved: hang 'em!
They said they were an-hungry; sigh'd forth proverbs,
That hunger broke stone walls; that dogs must eat;

---

   [14] *Fire* is here a dissyllable.   This and many other words, such as *hour*, *power*, *given*, &c., are used by the Poet as one or two syllables indifferently, to suit the metre.

   [15] *Ruth* is *pity* or *compassion :* a word little used now, but its sense survives in *ruthless*.

   [16] *Quarry*, or *querre*, signified slaughtered game of any kind; so called from being deposited in a square enclosed space in royal hunting.

   [17] *Pick* is an old form of *pitch*.   See *Henry VIII.*, page 172, note 21.

That meat was made for mouths ; that the gods sent not
Corn for the rich men only : with these shreds
They vented their complainings ; which being answer'd,
And a petition granted them, a strange one, —
To break the heart of generosity,[18]
And make bold power look pale, — they threw their caps
As they would hang them on the horns o' the Moon,
Shouting their emulation.[19]

  Men.   What is granted them?

  Mar. Five tribunes to defend their vulgar wisdoms,
Of their own choice : one's Junius Brutus, one
Sicinius Velutus, and I know not — 'Sdeath ![20]
The rabble should have first unroof'd the city,
Ere so prevail'd with me : it will in time
Win upon power, and throw forth greater themes
For insurrection's arguing.[21]

  Men.   This is strange.

  Mar. Go, get you home, you fragments ![22]

     Enter a Messenger, *hastily.*

  Mess. Where's Caius Marcius?

  Mar.   Here : what's the matter?

  Mess. The news is, sir, the Volsces are in arms.

  Mar. I'm glad on't ; then we shall ha' means to vent
Our musty superfluity. — See, our best elders !

---

[18] *Generosity*, in the sense of its Latin original, for *nobleness, high birth.*

[19] *Emulation*, here, is said to mean *factious contention.* I should rather explain it partisan rivalry ; trying who should shout the loudest.

[20] *'Sdeath !* is a disguised or softened oath, from *God's death.* So we have *'sblood*, *'slight*, *'sfoot*, and *zounds*, all formed in the same way ; *'slight* being from *God's light*, *zounds* from *God's wounds*, &c.

[21] That is, matter for insurrection to *lay hold of*, or *work upon.* So in *King Henry V.*, iii. 1 : " And sheath'd their swords for lack of *argument*."

[22] Fragments is *odds and ends*, or, as we say, *tag-rag.*

Enter COMINIUS, TITUS LARTIUS, *and other* Senators ; JUNIUS
BRUTUS *and* SICINIUS VELUTUS.

1 Sen. Marcius, 'tis true that you have lately told us ;
The Volsces are in arms.

Mar.   They have a leader,
Tullus Aufidius, that will put you to't.
I sin in envying his nobility ;
And, were I any thing but what I am,
I'd wish me only he.

Com.   You've fought together.

Mar. Were half to half the world by th' ears, and he
Upon my party, I'd revolt, to make
Only my wars with him : he is a lion
That I am proud to hunt.

1 Sen.   Then, worthy Marcius,
Attend upon Cominius to these wars.

Com. It is your former promise.

Mar.   Sir, it is ;
And I am constant. — Titus Lartius, thou
Shalt see me once more strike at Tullus' face.
What, art thou stiff ? stand'st out ?

Tit.   No, Caius Marcius ;
I'll lean upon one crutch, and fight with t'other,
Ere stay behind this business.

Men.   O, true-bred !

1 Sen. Your company to th' Capitol ; where, I know,
Our greatest friends attend us.

Tit. [*To* COM.]   Lead you on. —
[*To* MAR.] Follow Cominius : we must follow you ;
Right worthy you priority.[23]

---

[23] You *being* right worthy *of* priority or *precedence.*

Com.   Noble Marcius !

1 Sen. [*To the* Citizens.] Hence to your homes ; be
gone !

Mar.   Nay, let them follow.
The Volsces have much corn : take these rats thither
To gnaw their garners. — Worshipful mutineers,
Your valour puts well forth ; pray, follow.

            [*Exeunt all but* BRUTUS *and* SICINIUS. *The*
                         Citizens *steal away.*

Sic. Was ever man so proud as is this Marcius ?

Bru. He has no equal.

Sic. When we were chosen tribunes for the people, —

Bru. Mark'd you his lip and eyes ?

Sic.   Nay, but his taunts.

Bru. Being moved, he will not spare to gird [24] the gods.

Sic. Be-mock the modest Moon.

Bru. The present war devour him ! He is grown
Too proud to be so valiant.[25]

Sic.   Such a nature,
Tickled with good success,[26] disdains the shadow
Which he treads on at noon : but I do wonder
His insolence can brook to be commanded
Under Cominius.

Bru.   Fame, at the which he aims, —
In whom already he's well graced, — cannot

---

[24] A *gird* is a cut, a sarcasm, or stroke of satire.

[25] The first part of this speech is imprecative : "*May* the present war
devour him !" that is, *make an end* of him. — The latter part is an instance
of the infinitive used gerundively : "He is grown too proud *of being* so
valiant."

[26] *Success* means, literally, that which *follows* something else. Hence it
was formerly just as proper to say *bad* success as *good* success. *Sequel* and
sequent are now used in much the same way.

Better be held, nor more attain'd, than by
A place below the first : for what miscarries
Shall be the general's fault, though he perform
To th' utmost of a man ; and giddy censure
Will then cry out of Marcius, *O, if he*
Had borne the business !

 Sic.   ·   Besides, if things go well,
Opinion, that so sticks on Marcius, shall
Of his demerits [27] rob Cominius.

 Bru.   Come :
Half all Cominius' honours are to Marcius,
Though Marcius earn'd them not ; and all his faults
To Marcius shall be honours, though, indeed,
In aught he merit not.

 Sic.   Let's hence, and hear
How the dispatch is made ; and in what fashion,
More than his singularity,[28] he goes
Upon this present action.

 Bru.   Let's along.   *[Exeun*

SCENE II. — *Corioli.   The Senate-House.*

Enter TULLUS AUFIDIUS *and certain* Senators.

1 Sen. So, your opinion is, Aufidius,
That they of Rome are enter'd in [1] our counsels,
And know how we proceed.

---

[27] *Demerits* and *merits* had the same meaning. So in Cavendish's *Lif.*
of Wolsey : "I have not promoted you to condign preferments according
to your *demerits*." See *Othello*, page 58, note 8.

[28] That is, in what *style* or *character* other than his usual *assumption*, or
putting on airs, of superiority. Spoken sarcastically.

[1] *In* for *into ;* the two being often used indiscriminately.

Auf.   Is it not yours?
What ever hath been thought on in this State,
That could be brought to bodily act ere Rome
Had circumvention?[2] 'Tis not four days gone
Since I heard thence ; these are the words : I think
I have the letter here ; yes, here it is :

[Reads.] *They've press'd*[3] *a power, but it is not known*
Whether for east or west: the dearth is great;
The people mutinous; and it is rumour'd,
Cominius, Marcius your old enemy, —
Who is of Rome worse hated than of you, —
And Titus Lartius, a most valiant Roman,
These three lead on this preparation
Whither 'tis bent; most likely 'tis for you:
Consider of it.

1 Sen.   Our army's in the field :
We never yet made doubt but Rome was ready
To answer us.
    Auf.   Nor did you think it folly
To keep your great pretences[4] veil'd till when
They needs must show themselves ; which in the hatching,
It seem'd, appear'd to Rome.   By the discovery
We shall be shorten'd in our aim ; which was,

---

[2] That is, *underhand intelligence*, or *knowledge got by* circumvention.

[3] The use of *press'd* in this place is well explained by a passage in North's Plutarch : " The common people, being set on a broile and bravery with these words, would not appeare when the Consuls called their names by a bill, to *presse* them for the warres.   Martius then, who was now growne to great credit, and a stout man besides, rose up and openly spake against these flattering Tribunes : but to the warres the people by no means would be brought or *constrained*."

[4] *Pretences* is *intentions* or *purposes*.   See *Macbeth*, page 93, note 52.

To take-in [5] many towns, ere, almost, Rome
Should know we were afoot.

 2 Sen.   Noble Aufidius,
Take your commission ; hie you to your bands :
Let us alone to guard Corioli.
If they set down before's, for their remove
Bring up your army ; [6] but, I think, you'll find
They've not prepar'd for us.

 Auf.   O, doubt not that ;
I speak from certainties. Nay, more ;
Some parcels of their power are forth already,
And only hitherward. I leave your Honours.
If we and Caius Marcius chance to meet,
'Tis sworn between us, we shall ever strike
Till one can do no more. [7]

 All.   The gods assist you !
 Auf. And keep your Honours safe !
 1 Sen.   Farewell.
 2 Sen.   Farewell.
 All. Farewell.
           [*Exeunt.*

SCENE III. — *Rome.   A Room in* MARCIUS'S *House.*

Enter VOLUMNIA *and* VIRGILIA ; *they sit down on two low
stools, and sew.*

Vol. I pray you, daughter, sing ; or express yourself in a
more comfortable [1] sort : if my son were my husband, I

---

[5] To *take-in* was used for to *subdue*, to *conquer.*
[6] " If the Romans besiege us, bring up your army *to remove them.*"
[7] Keep on striking till one hath struck his last.
[1] *Comfortable* for *comforting*, that is, *cheerful ;* the passive form with the
active sense.   Repeatedly so.   See *King Lear*, page 91, note 36.

should freelier rejoice in that absence wherein he won
honour than in the embracements where he would show
most love.   When yet he was but tender-bodied, and
the only son of my womb; when youth with comeliness
pluck'd all gaze his way; when, for a day of kings' entreaties, a mother should not sell him an hour from her behold-
ing; I — considering how honour would become such a
person; that it was no better than picture-like to hang by
the wall, if renown made it not stir — was pleased to let him
seek danger where he was like to find fame.   To a cruel war
I sent him; from whence he return'd, his brows bound
with oak.   I tell thee, daughter, I sprang not more in joy
at first hearing he was a man-child than now in first seeing
he had proved himself a man.

Vir. But had he died in the business, madam, how then?

Vol. Then his good report should have been my son; I
therein would have found issue.   Hear me profess sincerely:
Had I a dozen sons, each in my love alike, and none less
dear than thine and my good Marcius, I had rather have
eleven die nobly for their country than one voluptuously
surfeit out of action.

Enter a Gentlewoman.

Gent. Madam, the Lady Valeria is come to visit you.

Vir. Beseech you, give me leave to retire[2] myself.

Vol. Indeed, you shall not.
Methinks I hear hither your husband's drum;
I see him pluck Aufidius down by th' hair;
As children from a bear, the Volsces shunning him:
Methinks I see him stamp thus, and call thus,
Come on, you cowards! you were got in fear,

---

[2] *Retire* in the sense of *withdraw;* a frequent usage.

Though you were born in Rome : his bloody brow
With his mail'd hand then wiping, forth he goes,
Like to a harvest-man, that's task'd to mow
Or all, or lose his hire.

Vir. His bloody brow ! O Jupiter, no blood !

Vol. Away, you fool ! it more becomes a man
Than gilt[3] his trophy : the breasts of Hecuba,
When she did suckle Hector, look'd not lovelier
Than Hector's forehead when it spit forth blood
At Grecian swords, contemning.[4] — Tell Valeria
We're fit to bid her welcome.   [*Exit* Gent.

Vir. Heavens bless my lord from fell Aufidius !

Vol. He'll beat Aufidius' head below his knee,
And tread upon his neck.

    Re-enter Gentlewoman *with* VALERIA *and her* Usher.

Val. My ladies both, good day to you.

Vol. Sweet madam.

Vir. I am glad to see your ladyship.

Val. How do you both? you're manifest house-keepers.[5]
What are you sewing here ? A fine spot,[6] in good faith.
How does your little son?

Vir. I thank your ladyship ; well, good madam.

Vol. He had rather see the swords, and hear a drum,
than look upon his schoolmaster.

Val. O' my word, the father's son : I'll swear, 'tis a very
pretty boy. O' my troth, I look'd upon him o' Wednesday

---

[3] *Gilt* was used for *gold* or *gilding*. So in *King Henry V.*, iv. 3: "Our gayness and our *gilt* are all besmirch'd."

[4] *Contemning* for *contemptuously* or *in contempt.*

[5] *House-keepers* for *home-keepers* or *stayers-at-home.*

[6] A handsome spot of embroidery. We often hear of *spotted* muslin.

half an hour together : 'has such a confirm'd countenance.
I saw him run after a gilded butterfly ; and, when he caught
it, he let it go again ; and after it again ; and over and over
he comes, and up again ; catch'd it again : and, whether his
fall enraged him, or how 'twas, he did so set his teeth, and
tear it ; O, I warrant, how he mammock'd[7] it !

Vol. One on's father's moods.

Val. Indeed, la, 'tis a noble child.

Vir. A crack,[8] madam.

Val. Come, lay aside your stitchery ; I must have you
play the idle huswife with me this afternoon.

Vir. No, good madam ; I will not out of doors.

Val. Not out of doors !

Vol. She shall, she shall.

Vir. Indeed, no, by your patience ; I'll not over the
threshold till my lord return from the wars.

Val. Fie, you confine yourself most unreasonably : come,
you must go visit the good lady that lies in.

Vir. I will wish her speedy strength, and visit her with
my prayers ; but I cannot go thither.

Vol. Why, I pray you?

Vir. 'Tis not to save labour, nor that I want love.

Val. You would be another Penelope : yet, they say, all
the yarn she spun in Ulysses' absence did but fill Ithaca full
of moths.   Come ; I would your cambric were sensible[9] as
your finger, that you might leave pricking it for pity.   Come,
you shall go with us.

---

7 To *mammock* is to tear or cut in pieces.

8 A *crack* is a sprightly forward boy.   So in Shallow's account of the
boy Jack Falstaff, *2 Henry IV.*, iii. 2: " I saw him break Skogan's head at
the court gate, when he was a *crack*, not thus high."

9 *Sensible* for *sensitive*, or *susceptible of pain.* See *Tempest*, page 83, note 26.

Vir. No, good madam, pardon me ; indeed, I will not forth.

Val. In, truth, la, go with me ; and I'll tell you excellent news of your husband.

Vir. O, good madam, there can be none yet.

Val. Verily, I do not jest with you ; there came news from him last night.

Vir. Indeed, madam?

Val. In earnest, it's true ; I heard a Senator speak it. Thus it is : The Volsces have an army forth ; against whom Cominius the general is gone, with one part of our Roman power : your lord and Titus Lartius are set down before their city Corioli ; they nothing doubt prevailing, and to make it brief wars. This is true, on mine honour ; and so, I pray, go with us.

Vir. Give me excuse, good madam ; I will obey you in every thing hereafter.

Vol. Let her alone, lady : as she is now, she will but disease our better mirth.

Val. In troth, I think she would. — Fare you well, then. — Come, good sweet lady. — Pr'ythee, Virgilia, turn thy solemness out o' door, and go along with us.

Vir. No, at a word, madam ; indeed, I must not. I wish you much mirth.

Val. Well, then, farewell. [*Exeunt.*

SCENE IV. — *Before Corioli.*

Enter, with drum and colours, MARCIUS, TITUS LARTIUS, Officers, *and* Soldiers.

Mar. Yonder comes news : a wager they have met.

Lart. My horse to yours, no.

Mar.   'Tis done.

Lart.   Agreed.

Enter a Messenger.

Mar. Say, has our general met the enemy?

Mess. They lie in view, but have not spoke as yet.[1]

Lart. So, the good horse is mine.

Mar.   I'll buy him of you.

Lart. No, I'll nor sell nor give him; lend you him I will

For half a hundred years. — Summon the town.

Mar. How far off lie these armies?

Mess.   Within this mile and half.

Mar. Then shall we hear their 'larum,[2] and they ours. —

Now, Mars, I pr'ythee, make us quick in work,

That we with smoking swords may march from hence,

To help our fielded friends![3] — Come, blow thy blast. —

They sound a parley. Enter, on the walls, some Senators *and others.*

Tullus Aufidius, is he within your walls?

1 Sen. No, nor a man that fears you more than he;

That's lesser than a little.   [*Drums afar off.*]   Hark, our drums

Are bringing forth our youth! we'll break our walls,

Rather than they shall pound us up: our gates,

Which yet seem shut, we have but pinn'd with rushes;

They'll open of themselves.   [*Alarum afar off.*]   Hark you, far off!

There is Aufidius; list, what work he makes

---

1 They lie in sight of each other, but have not yet given the signal of battle. See *Antony and Cleopatra*, page 72, note 23.

2 *Alarm* or *alarum* is, literally, *all arm;* the old cry, *To arms!*

3 Meaning, our friends who are in the field of battle.

Amongst your cloven army.

Mar.   O, they're at it !

Lart. Their noise be our instruction. — Ladders, ho !

The Volsces *enter and pass over.*

Mar. They fear us not, but issue forth their city.
Now put your shields before your hearts, and fight
With hearts more proof[4] than shields. — Advance, brave
    Titus :
They do disdain us much beyond our thoughts,
Which makes me sweat with wrath. — Come on, my fellows :
He that retires, I'll take him for a Volsce,
And he shall feel mine edge.

Alarum ; and exeunt Romans *and* Volsces, *fighting. The*
   Romans *are beaten back to their trenches. Re-enter* MAR-
   CIUS.

Mar. All the contagion of the south light on you,
You shames of Rome ! you herd of — Boils and plagues
Plaster you o'er ; that you may be abhorr'd
Further than seen, and one infect another
Against the wind a mile ! You souls of geese,
That bear the shapes of men, how have you run
From slaves that apes would beat ! Pluto and Hell !
All hurt behind ; backs red, and faces pale
With flight and agued fear ! Mend, and charge home,
Or, by the fires of heaven, I'll leave the foe,
And make my wars on you : look to't. Come on :
If you'll stand fast, we'll beat them to their wives,
As they us to our trenches. Follow me.

---

[4] *Proof,* as we still say *fire-proof,* or *reason-proof ;* proof *against fire,* or
against reason. The word is very common in the language of military
engineering.

Another alarum. The Volsces *and* Romans *re-enter, and*
  the fight is renewed. The Volsces *retire into Corioli, and*
  MARCIUS *follows them to the gates.*

So, now the gates are ope. Now prove good seconds:
'Tis for the followers fortune widens them,
Not for the fliers: mark me, and do the like.

  [Enters the gates.

 1 Sol. Fool-hardiness; not I.
 2 Sol. Nor I.   *[*MARCIUS *is shut in.*
 1 Sol. See, they have shut him in.
 All. To th' pot,[5] I warrant him. *[Alarum continues.*

   Re-enter TITUS LARTIUS.

 Lart. What is become of Marcius?
 All.   Slain, sir, doubtless.
 1 Sol. Following the fliers at the very heels,
With them he enters; who, upon the sudden,
Clapp'd-to their gates: he is himself alone,
To answer all the city.
 Lart.   O noble fellow!
Who, sensible,[6] outdares his senseless sword,
And, when it bows, stands up! Thou art lost, Marcius:
A carbuncle entire, as big as thou art,
Were not so rich a jewel. Thou wast a soldier
Even to Cato's wish,[7] not fierce and terrible

----

[5] That is, to the *pit* of destruction. "Gone to the *pot*" is still current,
though in rather vulgar language.

[6] *Sensible* is having *sensation.* See page 54, note 9. There is a similar
thought in Sidney's *Arcadia:* "Their very armour by piece-meale fell away
from them; yet their flesh abode the wounds constantly, as though it were
less *sensible* of smart than the senseless armour."

[7] So in North's Plutarch: "For he was even such another as Cato would
have a souldier and a captaine to be; not only terrible and fierce to lay

Only in strokes ; but, with thy grim looks and
The thunder-like percussion of thy sounds,
Thou madest thine enemies shake, as if the world
Were feverous and did tremble.

Re-enter MARCIUS, *bleeding, assaulted by the Enemy.*

1 Sol.   Look, sir.
Lart.   O, 'tis Marcius !
Let's fetch him off, or make remain [8] alike.

                     [They fight, and all enter the city.

SCENE V. — *Within Corioli.   A Street.*

Enter certain Romans, *with spoils.*

1 Rom. This will I carry to Rome.
2 Rom. And I this.
3 Rom. A murrain on't ! I took this for silver.

             [Alarum continues still afar off.

Enter MARCIUS *and* TITUS LARTIUS *with a* Trumpeter.

Mar. See here these movers that do prize their hours [1]
At a crack'd drachma !   Cushions, leaden spoons,
Irons of a doit,[2] doublets that hangmen would
Bury with those that wore them, these base slaves,

---

about him, but to make the enemy afeard with the sound of his voice and
grimnesse of his countenance." Cato was not born till some 255 years
after the death of Coriolanus. The Poet may have been led into the anachronism by not observing the difference between historical narrative and
dramatic representation.

  [8] *Make remain* sounds odd; but Shakespeare has many instances of the
word used in like manner.

  [1] *Hours* is here put for *time*, the most precious of all things in war.

  [2] Pieces of iron *not worth a copper.*

Ere yet the fight be done, pack up: down with them!
And hark, what noise the general makes!   To him!
There is the man of my soul's hate, Aufidius,
Piercing our Romans: then, valiant Titus, take
Convenient numbers to make good the city;
Whilst I, with those that have the spirit, will haste
To help Cominius.

    Lart.   Worthy sir, thou bleed'st;
Thy exercise hath been too violent for
A second course of fight.

    Mar.   Sir, praise me not;
My work hath yet not warm'd me: fare you well.
The blood I drop is rather physical [3]
Than dangerous to me: to Aufidius thus
I will appear, and fight.

    Lart.   Now the fair goddess, Fortune,
Fall deep in love with thee; and her great charms
Misguide th' opposers' swords!   Bold gentleman,
Prosperity be thy page!

    Mar.   Thy friend no less
Than those she placeth highest! [4]   So, farewell.

    Lart. Thou worthiest Marcius!—   *[Exit* MARCIUS.
Go, sound thy trumpet in the market-place;
Call thither all the officers o' the town,
Where they shall know our mind: away!   *[Exeunt.*

---

  [3] *Physical* for *wholesome* or *medicinal.* See *Julius Cæsar*, p. 86, note 52.
  [4] The meaning probably is, "Fortune, or prosperity, be thy friend no less than she is the friend of those whom she *holds dearest.*"

SCENE VI. — *Near the Camp of* COMINIUS.

Enter COMINIUS *and Forces, retreating.*

Com. Breathe you, my friends : well fought ; we are
    come off
Like Romans, neither foolish in our stands
Nor cowardly in retire : believe me, sirs,
We shall be charged again.   Whiles we have struck,
By interims and conveying gusts [1] we've heard
The charges of our friends. — Ye Roman gods,
Lead their successes as we wish our own,
That both our powers, with smiling fronts encountering,
May give you thankful sacrifice ! —

Enter a Messenger.

                    Thy news ?
Mess. The citizens of Corioli have issued,
And given to Lartius and to Marcius battle :
I saw our party to their trenches driven,
And then I came away.
Com.   Though thou speak'st truth,
Methinks thou speak'st not well.   How long is't since ?
Mess. Above an hour, my lord.
Com. 'Tis not a mile ; briefly, we heard their drums :
How couldst thou in a mile confound [2] an hour,
And bring thy news so late ?
Mess.   Spies of the Volsces

---

[1] Now and then, as gusts of wind conveyed the noise.
[2] To *confound* for to *consume* or *spend*.   Repeatedly so. — The sense of
the preceding clause appears to be, " in brief, the distance is so short, that
we heard their drums."

Held me in chase, that I was forced to wheel
Three or four miles about; else had I, sir,
Half an hour since brought my report.

   Com.   Who's yonder,
That does appear as he were flay'd? O gods!
He has the stamp of Marcius; and I have
Before-time seen him thus.

   Mar. [*Within.*]   Come I too late?

   Com. The shepherd knows not thunder from a tabor,
More than I know the sound of Marcius' tongue
From every meaner man's.

Enter MARCIUS.

   Mar.   Come I too late?

   Com. Ay, if you come not in the blood of others,
But mantled in your own.

   Mar.   O, let me clip ye
In arms as sound as when I woo'd; in heart
As merry as when our nuptial day was done,
And tapers burn'd to bedward!

   Com.   Flower of warriors,
How is't with Titus Lartius?

   Mar. As with a man busied about decrees:
Condemning some to death, and some to exile;
Ransoming him or pitying,[3] threatening th' other;
Holding Corioli in the name of Rome,
Even like a fawning greyhound in the leash,
To let him slip at will.

   Com.   Where is that slave

---

[3] Taking ransom of one, or letting him go for pity; treating with some
of the captives for the price of their freedom, or mercifully discharging them
without pay.

Which told me they had beat you to your trenches?
Where is he? call him hither.

Mar.   Let him alone;
He did inform the truth: but for our gentlemen,
The common file — a plague! — tribunes for them! —
The mouse ne'er shunn'd the cat as they did budge
From rascals worse than they.

Com.   But how prevail'd you?

Mar. Will the time serve to tell? I do not think so.
Where is the enemy? are you lords o' the field?
If not, why cease you till you are so?

Com.   Marcius,
We have at disadvantage fought, and did
Retire, to win our purpose.

Mar. How lies their battle?[4] know you on which side
They've placed their men of trust?

Com.   As I guess, Marcius,
Their bands i' the vaward are the Antiates,[5]
Of their best trust; o'er them Aufidius,
Their very heart of hope.

Mar.   I do beseech you,
By all the battles wherein we have fought,
By th' blood we've shed together, by the vows
We've made to endure friends, that you directly
Set me against Aufidius and his Antiates;
And that you not delay the present,[6] but,

---

[4] *Battle* was often used for *army;* especially of an army drawn up in battle-array, or an *embattled* army.

[5] The *vaward* is the *vanguard*, that is, the *front*, where the best soldiers would naturally be placed. — Shakespeare uses *Antiates* as a trisyllable, as if it had been written *Antiats*.

[6] Meaning the present *business;* that which craves instant dispatch.

Filling the air with swords advanced and darts,
We prove this very hour.

    Com.   Though I could wish
You were conducted to a gentle bath,
And balms applied to you, yet dare I never
Deny your asking : take your choice of those
That best can aid your action.

    Mar.   Those are they
That most are willing. — If any such be here —
As it were sin to doubt — that love this painting
Wherein you see me smear'd ; if any fear
Lesser his person [7] than an ill report ;
If any think brave death outweighs bad life,
And that his country's dearer than himself ;
Let him alone, or so many so minded,
Wave thus, t' express his disposition,
And follow Marcius.

       [*They all shout, and wave their swords ; take him
            up in their arms, and cast up their caps.*

Go we along ; make you a sword of me.
If these shows be not outward, which of you
But is four Volsces ? none of you but is
Able to bear against the great Aufidius
A shield as hard as his.   A certain number,
Though thanks to all, must I select : the rest
Shall bear the business in some other fight,
As cause will be obey'd.[8]   Please you to march ;
And I shall quickly draw out my command,

    [7] That is, fear less *for* his person.   Often so.   See *King Richard the Third*,
page 51, note 21.

    [8] As *occasion* shall *require.   Cause* and *occasion* readily interchange their
senses ; and the usage is common in all sorts of speech.

Which men are best inclined.[9]

Com.   March on, my fellows :
Make good this ostentation,[10] and you shall
Divide in all with us.   *[Exeunt.*

SCENE VII. — *The Gates of Corioli.*

TITUS LARTIUS, *having set a guard upon Corioli, going with
drum and trumpet toward* COMINIUS *and* CAIUS MARCIUS,
enters with a Lieutenant, *a party of* Soldiers, *and a*
Scout.

Lart. So, let the ports[1] be guarded : keep your duties,
As I have set them down. If I do send, dispatch
Those centuries[2] to our aid ; the rest will serve
For a short holding : if we lose the field,
We cannot keep the town.

Lieu.   Fear not our care, sir.

Lart. Hence, and shut your gates upon's. —
Our guider, come ; to th' Roman camp conduct us.

                                [Exeunt.

SCENE VIII. — *A Field of Battle between the Roman and
the Volscian Camps.*

Alarum. Enter, from opposite sides, MARCIUS *and* AUFIDIUS.

Mar. I'll fight with none but thee ; for I do hate thee
Worse than a promise-breaker.

---

[9] The order is, apparently, for the army to march along by him ; he the
while selecting such as seem fittest for the enterprise.

[10] This *showing* or *display of courage.* See *Much Ado,* page 97, note 9.

[1] The *ports* are the *gates.* Like the Latin *porta.*

[2] *Centuries* are companies of a hundred men each.

Auf.   We hate alike :
Not Afric owns a serpent I abhor
More than thy fame I envy.   Fix thy foot.

  Mar. Let the first budger die the other's slave,
And the gods doom him after !

  Auf.   If I fly, Marcius,
Halloo me like a hare.

  Mar.   Within these three hours, Tullus,
Alone I fought in your Corioli walls,
And made what work I pleased : 'tis not my blood
Wherein thou see'st me mask'd ; for thy revenge
Wrench up thy power to th' highest.

  Auf.   Wert thou the Hector
That was the whip of your bragg'd progeny,[3]
Thou shouldst not 'scape me here. —

                    [*They fight, and certain* Volsces *come to*
                                the aid of AUFIDIUS.

Officious, and not valiant, you have shamed me
In your condemnèd seconds.[4]

                    [*Exeunt fighting, driven in by* MARCIUS.

        SCENE IX. — *The Roman Camp.*

*Alarum. A retreat is sounded. Flourish. Enter, from
    one side,* COMINIUS *and* Romans ; *from the other side,*
    MARCIUS, *with his arm in a scarf, and other* Romans.

  Com. If I should tell thee o'er this thy day's work,
Thou'lt not believe thy deeds : but I'll report it,

    [3] The whip or *scourge* that your boasted *progenitors* were possessed of.
This use of *progeny* for *progenitors* is, I believe, singular.
    [4] *Condemnèd seconds* is *help* condemned *as worthless or unavailing.* The
use of to *second* for to *help* is very common.

Where Senators shall mingle tears with smiles ;
Where great patricians shall attend, and shrug,
I' the end admire ; where ladies shall be frighted,
And, gladly quaked,[1] hear more ; where the dull tribunes,
That, with the fusty plébeians,[2] hate thine honours,
Shall say, against their hearts, *We thank the gods
Our Rome hath such a soldier !*
Yet camest thou to a morsel of this feast,[3]
Having fully dined before.

  Enter TITUS LARTIUS, *with his power, from the pursuit.*

 Lart.   O general,
Here is the steed, we the caparison :
Hadst thou beheld —
 Mar.   Pray now, no more : my mother,
Who has a charter[4] to extol her blood,
When she does praise me grieves me.   I have done
As you have done, — that's what I can ; induced
As you have been, — that's for my country :
He that has but effected his good will
Hath overta'en mine act.
 Com.   You shall not be
The grave of your deserving ; Rome must know
The value of her own : 'twere a concealment
Worse than a theft, no less than a traducement,
To hide your doings ; and to silence that

---

 1 " Gladly *quaked*" is gladly *made to tremble*, or to *shake*, with fright.
 2 Shakespeare repeatedly uses *plebeians* with the first syllable accented,
as if it were spelt *plebeans*.
 3 We should say "*this* morsel of *a* feast."   The meaning is, that what
the hero has done here is but as a morsel, *compared to* the full meal of
fighting which he had before gone through at Corioli.
 4 *Charter* is *special privilege* or *admitted right*.

Which, to the spire and top of praises vouch'd,
Would seem but modest : [5] therefore, I beseech you —
In sign of what you are, not to reward
What you have done — before our army hear me.

   Mar. I have some wounds upon me, and they smart
To hear [6] themselves remember'd.

   Com.   Should they not,
Well might they fester 'gainst ingratitude,
And tent [7] themselves with death.   Of all the horses, —
Whereof we've ta'en good, and good store, — of all
The treasure in this field achieved and city,
We render you the tenth ; to be ta'en forth,
Before the common distribution, at
Your only choice.

   Mar.   I thank you, general ;
But cannot make my heart consent to take
A bribe to pay my sword : I do refuse it ;
And stand upon my common part with those
That have beheld the doing.

        [*A long flourish.   They all cry*, Marcius ! Marcius !
           cast up their caps and lances: COMINIUS *and*
           LARTIUS *stand bare.*

   Mar. May these same instruments, which you profane,
Never sound more !   Shall drums and trumpets, when
I' the field, prove flatterers?   Let Courts and cities be
Made all of false-faced soothing, where steel grows

---

   [5] An irregular construction ; but the meaning is, " It were no less than a
slander, to pass silently over that prowess which might be praised to the
utmost, and still the praise would come short of the truth."

   [6] *To hear* is equivalent to *at hearing*.   See page 48, note 25.

   [7] To *tent* a wound is, properly, to *probe* it : here the word is used in the
general sense of to *dress*, or to *heal*.

Soft as the parasite's silk : let them be made
An overture for th' wars.[8]   No more, I say !
For that I have not wash'd my nose that bled,
Or foil'd some debile wretch, — which, without note,
Here's many else have done, — you shout me forth
In acclamations hyperbolical ;
As if I loved my little should be dieted
In praises sauced with lies.
 Com.   Too modest are you ;
More cruel to your good report than grateful
To us that give you truly : by your patience,
If 'gainst yourself you be incensed, we'll put you —
Like one that means his proper harm — in manacles,
Then reason [9] safely with you. — Therefore, be't known,
As to us, to all the world, that Caius Marcius
Wears this war's garland : in token of the which,
My noble steed, known to the camp, I give him,
With all his trim belonging ; and from this time,
For what he did before Corioli, call him,
With all th' applause and clamour of the host,
CAIUS MARCIUS CORIOLANUS. — Bear
Th' addition nobly ever !
       [*Flourish.   Trumpets sound and drums.*

---

[8] That is, let drums and trumpets be used in making *introductions* or
preludes to battle. As to the meaning of the whole passage, it may be
observed that the speaker is referring to the "long flourish" which has
just been made with the instruments in honour of what he has done. This
he regards as a profanation : he would have drums and trumpets used only
for sounding incitements to valiant action, not for sounding compliments
and flatteries on the battle-field. All such "false-faced soothing" he would
have confined to " Courts and cities," where steel itself, like silk, is used for
ornament, not for fighting.

[9] To *reason*, as the word is here used, is to *talk* or *converse*. Often so.

All. Caius Marcius Coriolanus !

Cor. I will go wash ;
And, when my face is fair, you shall perceive
Whether I blush or no : howbeit, I thank you. —
I mean to stride your steed ; and at all times,
To undercrest your good addition
To th' fairness of my power.[10]

Com.   So, to our tent ;
Where, ere we do repose us, we will write
To Rome of our success. — You, Titus Lartius,
Must to Corioli back : send us to Rome
The best, with whom we may articulate,[11]
For their own good and ours.

Lart.   I shall, my lord.

Cor. The gods begin to mock me.   I, that now
Refused most princely gifts, am bound to beg
Of my lord general.

Com.   Take't ; 'tis yours.   What is't?

Cor. I sometime lay, here in Corioli,
At a poor man's house ; he used me kindly.
He cried to me ; I saw him prisoner ;
But then Aufidius was within my view,
And wrath o'erwhelm'd my pity : I request you
To give my poor host freedom.[12]

---

[10] *Addition* is *title ;* the monumental surname just conferred upon him. To *undercrest* is to *sustain,* to *bear ;* as a man bears his helmet, or the distinctive badge worn upon it. So that the meaning is, " I will support, as fairly as I can, the honourable distinction you have bestowed upon me."

[11] The *chief men* of Corioli, with whom we may *enter into articles.* Bullokar has the word " *articulate,* to set down articles, or conditions of agreement." We still retain the word *capitulate,* which anciently had nearly the same meaning, namely, " To *article,* or agree upon articles."

[12] The Poet found this incident thus related in Plutarch : " Onely this

Com.　　　　　　　　　　　O, well begg'd !
Were he the butcher of my son, he should
Be free as is the wind. — Deliver him, Titus.

Lart. Marcius, his name?

Cor.　　　　　　　　By Jupiter, forgot !
I'm weary ; yea, my memory is tired. —
Have we no wine here?

Com.　　　　　　　Go we to our tent :
The blood upon your visage dries ; 'tis time
It should be look'd to : come.　　　　　*[Exeunt.*

SCENE X. — *The Camp of the* Volsces.

A flourish.　　Cornets.　　Enter TULLUS AUFIDIUS *bloody, with
two or three* Soldiers.

Auf. The town is ta'en !

1 Sol. 'Twill be deliver'd back on good condition.

Auf. Condition !
I would I were a Roman ; for I cannot,
Being a Volsce, be that I am.[1]　Condition !
What good condition can a treaty find
I' the part that is at mercy? — Five times, Marcius,
I've fought with thee ; so often hast thou beat me ;
And wouldst do so, I think, should we encounter

grace, said he, I crave, and beseech you to grant me : Among the Volsces
there is an old friend and hoast of mine, an honest wealthy man, and now a
prisoner ; who, living before in great wealth in his owne countrey, liveth now
a poore prisoner in the hands of his enemies ; and yet, notwithstanding all
this his misery and misfortune, it would do me great pleasure, if I could
save him from this one danger, to keepe him from being sold as a slave."

[1] "If I were a Roman, I could love Marcius as a compatriot and friend ;
but, being a Volsce, I cannot remain true to myself ; my hatred of him as
an enemy is transforming me from what I rightly am into a villain."

As often as we eat. — By th' elements,
If e'er again I meet him beard to beard,
He's mine, or I am his : mine emulation
Hath not that honour in't it had ; for, where [2]
I thought to crush him in an equal force,
True sword to sword, I'll poach [3] at him some way,
Or wrath or craft may get him.

 1 Sol.   He's the Devil.

 Auf. Bolder, though not so subtle. My valour, poison'd
With only suffering stain by him, for him
Shall fly out of itself : [4] nor sleep nor sanctuary,
Being naked, sick ; nor fane nor Capitol,
The prayers of priests nor times of sacrifice,
Embankments all of fury, shall lift up
Their rotten privilege and custom 'gainst
My hate to Marcius : where I find him, were it
At home, upon my brother's guard, [5] even there,
Against the hospitable canon, [6] would I

 [2] *Where* for *whereas* again. See page 41, note 7.

 [3] To *poach* is to thrust at with a sharp-pointed instrument. Thus in Carew's *Survey of Cornwall*, speaking of fish : " They use to *poche* them with an instrument somewhat like a salmon-speare."

 [4] " My valour, to reach his life, shall lose its nature, cease to be generous in respect of time and means." — In the next line, the meaning is, " *he* being naked, sick."

 [5] That is, in my own house under my brother's protection. — Upon this speech of Aufidius, Coleridge remarks as follows : " I have such deep faith in Shakespeare's heart-lore, that I take for granted that this is in nature ; although I cannot in myself discover any germ of possible feeling, which could wax and unfold itself into such a sentiment. However, I perceive that in this speech is meant to be contained a prevention of shock at the after-change in Aufidius' character."

 [6] " The hospitable canon " is the law or obligation of hospitality. In the Roman code of morals, the person of a guest was sacred.

Wash my fierce hand in's heart.　Go you to th' city;
Learn how 'tis held; and what they are that must
Be hostages for Rome.

　　1 Sol.　　　　　　　Will not you go?

　　Auf.　I am attended[7] at the cypress grove : I pray you,—
'Tis south the city mills,—bring me word thither
How the world goes, that to the pace of it
I may spur on my journey.

　　1 Sol.　　　　　　　I shall, sir.　　　　*[Exeunt.*

ACT II.

Scene I. — *Rome.　A public Place.*

Enter Menenius, Sicinius, *and* Brutus.

Men.　The augurer tells me we shall have news to-night.

Bru.　Good or bad?

Men.　Not according to the prayer of the people, for they
love not Marcius.

Sic.　Nature teaches beasts to know their friends.

Men.　Pray you, whom does the wolf love?

Sic.　The lamb.

Men.　Ay, to devour him; as the hungry plebeians would
the noble Marcius.

Bru.　He's a lamb indeed, that baes like a bear.

Men.　He's a bear indeed, that lives like a lamb.　You
two are old men: tell me one thing that I shall ask you.

Both.　Well, sir.

----

[7] *Attended* here means *waited for*.　See *Cymbeline*, page 152, note 36.

Men. In what enormity is Marcius poor in,[1] that you two have not in abundance?

Bru. He's poor in no one fault, but stored with all.

Sic. Especially in pride.

Bru. And topping[2] all others in boasting.

Men. This is strange now. Do you two know how you are censured here in the city, I mean of us o' the right-hand file? do you?

Both. Why, how are we censured?

Men. Because you talk of pride now, — will you not be angry?

Both. Well, well, sir, well.

Men. Why, 'tis no great matter; for a very little thief of occasion will rob you of a great deal of patience: give your dispositions the reins, and be angry at your pleasures; at the least, if you take it as a pleasure to you in being so. You blame Marcius for being proud?

Bru. We do it not alone, sir.

Men. I know you can do very little alone; for your helps are many, or else your actions would grow wondrous single :[3] your abilities are too infant-like for doing much alone. You talk of pride : O that you could turn your eyes toward the napes of your necks,[4] and make but an interior survey of your good selves ! O that you could !

Bru. What then, sir?

Men. Why, then you should discover a brace of unmerit-

---

1 This doubling of the preposition was common. See *Romeo and Juliet*, page 66, note 18.

2 To *top* is to *surpass;* a frequent usage. See *Macbeth*, page 137, note 10.

3 The Poet repeatedly uses *single* for *weak* or *feeble*.

4 Alluding to the fable, that every man has a bag hanging before him, in which he puts his neighbour's faults; and another behind, for his own.

ing, proud, violent, testy magistrates, *alias* fools, as any in Rome.

Sic. Menenius, you are known well enough too.

Men. I am known to be a humorous patrician, and one that loves a cup of hot wine with not a drop of allaying Tiber in't ;[5] said to be something imperfect in favouring the thirst complaint ; hasty and tinder-like upon too trivial motion ; one that converses more with the latter end of the night than with the forehead of the morning :[6] what I think I utter, and spend my malice in my breath. Meeting two such wealsmen as you are, — I cannot call you Lycurguses, — if the drink you give me touch my palate adversely, I make a crooked face at it. I cannot say your Worships have deliver'd the matter well, when I find the ass in compound with the major part of your syllables : and though I must be content to bear with those that say you are reverend grave men, yet they lie deadly that tell you you have good faces. If you see this in the map of my microcosm,[7] follows it that I am known well enough too ? what harm can your bisson[8] conspectuities glean out of this character, if I be known well enough too ?

---

[5] We have a similar expression in Lovelace's song, *To Althea, from Prison:*

> When flowing cups run swiftly round,
>   With no *allaying Thames ;*
> Our careless heads with roses bound,
>   Our hearts with loyal flames.

[6] Rather a late lier-down than an early riser. So in *Love's Labours Lost :* "In the *posteriors* of this day, which the rude multitude call the afternoon."

[7] This word is well explained in Raleigh's *History of the World :* "Because, in the little frame of man's body, there is a representation of the universal, and (by allusion) a participation of all the parts there, therefore man was called *microcosmos*, or *the little world*."

[8] *Bisson* is an old word for *blind.* So in Udal, St. Mark, viii.: "Thys manne was not purblynde, or a lyttle appayred and decayed in syght, but

Bru. Come, sir, come, we know you well enough.

Men. You know neither me, yourselves, nor any thing. You are ambitious for poor knaves' caps and legs : [9] you wear out a good wholesome forenoon in hearing a cause between an orange-wife and a fosset-seller ; and then rejourn the controversy of three-pence to a second day of audience. When you are hearing a matter between party and party, if you chance to be pinch'd with the colic, you make faces like mummers ; set up the bloody flag against all patience ; [10] and dismiss the controversy bleeding, the more entangled by your hearing : all the peace you make in their cause is, calling both the parties knaves. You are a pair of strange ones.

Bru. Come, come, you are well understood to be a perfecter giber for the table than a necessary bencher in the Capitol.

Men. Our very priests must become mockers, if they shall encounter such ridiculous subjects as you are. [11] When you speak best unto the purpose, it is not worth the wagging of your beards ; and your beards deserve not so honourable a grave as to stuff a botcher's cushion, or to be entomb'd in an ass's pack-saddle. Yet you must be saying, Marcius is proud ; who, in a cheap estimation, is worth all your predecessors since Deucalion ; though peradventure some of the best of 'em were hereditary hangmen. God-den [12] to your

---

as *bysome* as was possible to be." The word was variously spelt *bizend, beesen, bison.* It is hardly needful to add that "bisson conspectuities" is a humorous substitute for *blind eyes.* See *Hamlet,* page 119, note 83.

[9] For their obeisance; called *making a leg.* See The First Part of *King Henry the Fourth,* page 114, note 47.

[10] Declare war against patience.

[11] So in *Much Ado about Nothing :* "Courtesy itself must convert to disdain, if you come in her presence."

[12] *God-den* is an old colloquialism for *good even* or *good day.*

Worships : more of your conversation would infect my brain, being the herdsmen of the beastly plebeians : I will be bold to take my leave of you. — [BRUTUS *and* SICINIUS *retire.*

Enter VOLUMNIA, VIRGILIA, *and* VALERIA, *with* Attendants.

How now, my as fair as noble ladies, — and the Moon, were she earthly, no nobler, — whither do you follow your eyes so fast ?

Vol. Honourable Menenius, my boy Marcius approaches ; for the love of Juno, let's go.

Men. Ha ! Marcius coming home ?

Vol. Ay, worthy Menenius ; and with most prosperous approbation.

Men. Take my cap, Jupiter, and I thank thee. — Hoo ! Marcius coming home !

Vir. } Nay, 'tis true.
Val. }

Vol. Look, here's a letter from him : the State hath another, his wife another ; and, I think, there's one at home for you.

Men. I will make my very house reel to-night. A letter for me !

Vir. Yes, certain, there's a letter for you ; I saw't.

Men. A letter for me ! it gives me an estate of seven years' health ; in which time I will make a lip at the physician : the most sovereign prescription in Galen is but empiricutic,[13] and, to [14] this preservative, of no better report than

---

[13] A word probably coined by old Menenius himself for *quack medicine.* — Divers critics have made merry at the Poet for thus making Menenius refer to Galen, the person speaking having lived about 650 years before the person spoken of. I leave it for others to determine whether the anachronism were perpetrated in ignorance or in contempt of historical accuracy.

[14] *Compared to,* or *in comparison with. To* is often used thus.

a horse-drench.   Is he not wounded? he was wont to come home wounded.

Vir.   O, no, no, no.

Vol.   O, he is wounded; I thank the gods for't.

Men.   So do I too, if it be not too much.   Brings 'a victory in his pocket?   The wounds become him.

Vol.   On's brows: [15] Menenius, he comes the third time home with the oaken garland.

Men.   Has he disciplined Aufidius soundly?

Vol.   Titus Lartius writes, they fought together, but Aufidius got off.

Men.   And 'twas time for him too, I'll warrant him that: an he had stay'd by him, I would not have been so fidius'd for all the chests in Corioli, and the gold that's in them.   Is the Senate possess'd [16] of this?

Vol.   Good ladies, let's go. — Yes, yes, yes; the Senate has letters from the general, wherein he gives my son the whole name of the war: he hath in this action outdone his former deeds doubly.

Val.   In troth, there's wonderous things spoke of him.

Men.   Wondrous! ay, I warrant you, and not without his true purchasing.

Vir.   The gods grant them true!

Vol.   True! pow, wow.

Men.   True! I'll be sworn they are true.   Where is he wounded? — [*To the* Tribunes.]   God save your good Worships!   Marcius is coming home: he has more cause to be proud. — Where is he wounded?

---

[15] "*He brings victory on* his brow"; for he comes the third time home *brow-bound* with the *oaken garland*. Volumnia's thoughts stick upon Menenius's question, "Brings 'a victory in his pocket?" and she takes no notice of the words, "The wounds become him."

[16] *Possess'd* is *informed*. See *Twelfth Night*, page 65, note 25.

Vol. I' the shoulder and i' the left arm : there will be large cicatrices to show the people, when he shall stand for his place. He received in the repulse of Tarquin seven hurts i' the body.

Men. One i' the neck, and two i' the thigh ; there's nine that I know.[17]

Vol. He had, before this last expedition, twenty-five wounds upon him.

Men. Now it's twenty-seven : every gash was an enemy's grave. [*A shout and flourish within.*] Hark ! the trumpets.

Vol. These are the ushers of Marcius : before him he carries noise, and behind him he leaves tears.

*Death, that dark spirit, in's nervy arm doth lie ;
*Which being advanced, declines, and then men die.[18]

A sennet. Trumpets sound. Enter COMINIUS *and* TITUS LARTIUS ; *between them,* CORIOLANUS, *crowned with an oaken garland ; with* Captains, Soldiers, *and a* Herald.

Her. Know, Rome, that all alone Marcius did fight
Within Corioli gates ; where he hath won,
With fame, a name to [19] *Caius Marcius ;* these
In honour follows *Coriolanus.* — Welcome,
Welcome to Rome, renown'd Coriolanus !　　　[*Flourish.*

---

[17] Menenius probably has no reference to the wounds that Volumnia was speaking of, but is trying to reckon up and locate those already known to himself : he therefore specifies three, and then, in his haste, merely states the gross number.

[18] He has but to lift up his hand, and let it fall, and men sink beneath it. — This ranting couplet is most likely an interpolation ; perhaps, as White thinks, " added in the prompter's book, to please the actor of *Volumnia* with a round, mouth-filling speech."

[19] Here *to* has the force of *in addition to.* See *Macbeth*, page 99, note 9.

All. Welcome to Rome, renown'd Coriolanus!

Cor. No more of this, it does offend my heart;
Pray now, no more.

Com.   Look, sir, your mother:

Cor.   O,
You have, I know, petition'd all the gods
For my prosperity.   [*Kneels.*

Vol. [*Raising him.*] Nay, my good soldier, up;
My gentle Marcius, worthy Caius, and
By deed-achieving honour newly named, —
What is it? — Coriolanus must I call thee?
But, O, thy wife!

Cor.   My gracious silence, hail![20]
Wouldst thou have laugh'd had I come coffin'd home,
That weep'st to see me triumph? Ah, my dear,
Such eyes the widows in Corioli wear,
And mothers that lack sons.

Men.   Now, the gods crown thee!

Cor. And live you yet? — [*To* VALERIA.] O my sweet
          lady, pardon.

Vol. I know not where to turn. — O, welcome home! —
And welcome, general! and ye're welcome all.

Men. A hundred thousand welcomes: — I could weep,
And I could laugh; I'm light and heavy: — welcome!
A curse begin at very root on's heart
That is not glad to see thee! — You are three
That Rome should dote on: yet, by th' faith of men,

---

[20] By "gracious silence" is probably meant, "thou whose silent tears
are more eloquent and grateful to me than the clamorous applause of the rest."
So in Jonson's *Every Man Out of his Humour :* "You shall see sweet *silent
rhetoric* and *dumb eloquence* speaking in her eye." *Gracious* is sometimes
used by Shakespeare for *grateful, acceptable.*

We've some old crab-trees here at home that will not
Be grafted to your relish.   Yet welcome, warriors !
We call a nettle but a nettle, and
The faults of fools but folly.

    Com.   Ever right.

    Cor. Menenius ever, ever.

    Her. Give way there, and go on !

    Cor. [*To* Vol. *and* Vir.]   Your hand, and yours :
Ere in our own house I do shade my head,
The good patricians must be visited ;
From whom I have received not only greetings,
But with them charge of honours.

    Vol.   I have lived
To see inherited my very wishes,[21]
And the buildings of my fancy : only there
Is one thing wanting, which I doubt not but
Our Rome will cast upon thee.

    Cor.   Know, good mother,
I had rather be their servant in my way
Than sway with them in theirs.

    Com.   On, to the Capitol !

       [*Flourish.   Cornets.   Exeunt in state, as before.*
               Brutus *and* Sicinius *come forward.*

    Bru. All tongues speak of him, and the blearèd sights
Are spectacled to see him : your prattling nurse
Into a rupture lets her baby cry
While she chats him :[22] the kitchen malkin pins

---

    [21] "To see myself *in possession* of all I have wished for." The use of
inherit for *possess* or *have* occurs frequently. See *Tempest*, p. 125, note 30.

    [22] "While she chats him" probably means "while she *makes* him the
theme of chat; she being so carried away with the enthusiasm as to lose all
thought of the crying baby, cry he never so vehemently.— It having been

Her richest lockram 'bout her reechy neck,[23]
Clambering the walls to eye him : stalls, bulks, windows,
Are smother'd up, leads fill'd, and ridges horsed [24]
With variable complexions ; all agreeing
In earnestness to see him : seld-shown flamens
Do press among the popular throngs, and puff
To win a vulgar station : [25] our veil'd dames
Commit the war of white and damask, in
Their nicely-gauded cheeks, to th' wanton spoil
Of Phœbus' burning kisses : such a pother,
As if that whatsoever god who leads him
Were slily crept into his human powers,
And gave him graceful posture.

   Sic.   On the sudden,
I warrant him Consul.

questioned whether crying ever causes a rupture in babies, Judge Black-stone said, " I have inquired, and am told it is usual." Whereupon Dr. C. M. Ingleby observes, " Probably most fathers and mothers know that such is the fact." And he quotes from Phioravante's *Secrets*, 1582 : " To helpe yong Children of the Rupture. The Rupture is caused two waies, the one through weaknesse of the place, and the other through much criyng."

[23] " Kitchen *malkin* " is equivalent to kitchen *wench*, as " country *mal-kin* " is to country *wench*. *Malkin*, applied to a woman, is of frequent occur-rence in old writers, and is supposed to be a diminutive of *Mal*, that is *Mary*, as *Wilkin* is of *Will*, and *Tomkin* of *Tom.* — *Lockram* was a cheap coarse linen. — *Reechy* is *reeking*, that is, *smoky*. So in *The Invisible Comedy*, 1610 : " He look'd so *reechily*, like bacon hanging on the chimney's roof."

[24] Men crowd together upon the lead-covered roofs, and sit astride the ridge-poles, of houses.

[25] *Seld* was often used for *seldom*. Flamens were a high order of priests. — " Vulgar station " is a standing-place among the vulgar. — A *war of colours* in a woman's face seems to have been a favourite image with the Poet. So in *The Taming of the Shrew :* " Such *war of white and red* within her cheeks." And in *Lucrece :*

> The silent *war* of lilies and of roses,
> Which Tarquin view'd in her fair face's field.

Bru.   Then our office may,
During his power, go sleep.

Sic. He cannot temperately transport his honours
From where he should begin to th' end ; but will
Lose those he hath won.[26]

Bru.   In that there's comfort.

Sic.   Doubt not
The commoners, for whom we stand, but they,
Upon their ancient malice, will forget,
With the least cause, these his new honours ; which
That he will give them, make as little question
As he is proud to do't.[27]

Bru.   I heard him swear,
Were he to stand for Consul, never would he
Appear i' the market-place, nor on him put
The napless vesture of humility ;
Nor, showing, as the manner is, his wounds
To th' people, beg their stinking breaths.

Sic.   'Tis right.

Bru. It was his word : O, he would miss it, rather
Than carry't but by th' suit o' the gentry to him,
And the desire of the nobles.

Sic.   I wish no better
Than have him hold that purpose, and to put it
In execution.

Bru.   'Tis most like he will.

---

[26] The meaning seems to be, he cannot be content to proceed temperately in the course of honour, beginning, as he should, with the lower, and
advancing gradually to the highest : and so will make shipwreck of all his
honours by the way.

[27] "Which *cause* make as little question that he will give them as *that* he
is *proud of doing* it." "Proud *to do't*" is another instance of the infinitive
used gerundively.

Sic. It shall be to him, then, as our good wills,[28]
A sure destruction.

Bru.   So it must fall out
To him or our authorities.   For an end,
We must suggest the people in what hatred
He still hath held them ; that to's power [29] he would
Have made them mules, silenced their pleaders, and
Dispropertied their freedoms ; holding them,
In human action and capacity,
Of no more soul nor fitness for the world
Than camels in the war ; who have their provand [30]
Only for bearing burdens, and sore blows
For sinking under them.

Sic.   This, as you say, suggested
At some time when his soaring insolence
Shall touch the people, — which time shall not want,
If he be put upon't ; and that's as easy
As to set dogs on sheep, — will be as fire
To kindle their dry stubble ; and their blaze
Shall darken him for ever. —

Enter a Messenger.

Bru.   What's the matter?
Mess. You're sent for to the Capitol.   'Tis thought
That Marcius shall be Consul.
I've seen the dumb men throng to see him, and
The blind to hear him speak : matrons flung gloves,
Ladies and maids their scarfs and handkerchers,

---

28 As our *interest requires ; wills* being a verb.
29 Meaning, to *the utmost* of his power.
30 *Provand* is an old word for *provender.*

Upon him as he pass'd : [31] the nobles bended,
As to Jove's statue ; and the commons made
A shower and thunder with their caps and shouts.
I never saw the like.

 Bru.   Let's to the Capitol ;
And carry with us ears and eyes for th' time,
But hearts for the event.

 Sic.   Have with you.   [*Exeunt.*

SCENE II. — *The Same. The Capitol.*

Enter two Officers, *to lay cushions.*

 1 Off. Come, come, they are almost here. How many stand for consulships?

 2 Off. Three, they say : but 'tis thought of every one Coriolanus will carry it.

 1 Off. That's a brave fellow ; but he's vengeance proud, and loves not the common people.

 2 Off. Faith, there have been many great men that have flatter'd the people, who ne'er loved them ; and there be many that they have loved, they know not wherefore : so that, if they love they know not why, they hate upon no better a ground : therefore, for Coriolanus neither to care whether they love or hate him manifests the true knowledge he has in their disposition ; and, out of his noble carelessness, lets them plainly see't.

 1 Off. If he did not care whether he had their love or no, he'd waved indifferently 'twixt doing them neither good

---

[31] Another anachronism ; the Romans being represented as doing what, in the days of chivalry, was done at tiltings and tournaments in honour of the successful combatant.

nor harm ; but he seeks their hate with greater devotion than they can render it him, and leaves nothing undone that may fully discover him their opposite. Now, to seem to affect the malice and displeasure of the people is as bad as that which he dislikes, to flatter them for their love.

2 Off. He hath deserved worthily of his country : and his ascent is not by such easy degrees as those who,[1] having been supple and courteous to the people, bonneted into their estimation and report, without any further deed to have them at all :[2] but he hath so planted his honours in their eyes, and his actions in their hearts, that for their tongues to be silent, and not confess so much, were a kind of ingrateful injury ; to report otherwise, were a malice, that, giving itself the lie, would pluck reproof and rebuke from every ear that heard it.

1 Off. No more of him ; he's a worthy man : make way, they are coming.

A sennet. Enter, with Lictors *before them,* COMINIUS, ME-NENIUS, CORIOLANUS, Senators, SICINIUS, *and* BRUTUS. *The* Senators *take their places; the* Tribunes *take theirs also by themselves.*

1 Properly it should be "as *theirs* who"; but the Poet has many like instances of loose construction. Here the irregularity does not obscure the sense.

2 The meaning is, won the favour of the people by pulling off the hat to them, without doing any thing further to earn it. This is the explanation given by Delius, and is surely right. To *bonnet* or to *cap* is to uncover the head as a token or ceremony of respect. So in *Othello*, i. 1 : "Three great ones of the city, in personal suit to make me his lieutenant, oft *capp'd* to him." See, also, *Othello*, page 58, note 8. — Political demagogues are the same in all ages, evermore fawning and toadying their way into popular favour, and eating all sorts of dirt to the people in order to get their votes; and the people *love to have it so :* all which we need not go far to learn. See Critical Notes.

Men. Having determined of the Volsces, and
To send for Titus Lartius, it remains,
As the main point of this our after-meeting,
To gratify his noble service that
Hath thus stood for his country : therefore, please you,
Most reverend and grave elders, to desire
The present Consul, and last general
In our well-found successes, to report
A little of that worthy work perform'd
By Caius Marcius Coriolanus ; whom
We meet here, both to thank, and to remember
With honours like himself.[3]

1 Sen.   Speak, good Cominius :
Leave nothing out for length, and make us think
Rather our State's defective for requital
Than we to stretch it out. — [*To the* Tribunes.] Masters o'
        the people,
We do request your kindest ears ; and, after,
Your loving motion toward the common body,
To yield what passes here.

Sic.   We are convented
Upon a pleasing treaty ; and have hearts
Inclinable[4] to honour and advance
The theme of our assembly.

Bru.   Which the rather

---

[3] "With honours *like himself*" probably means with honours *suited or
proportionable to his merits.* — "*For* length," in the next line is *on account
of* length. So in i. 10, of this play : "My valour, poison'd with only suffering stain by him, *for him* shall fly out of itself." See, also, *Macbeth*, page
103, note 22.

[4] *Inclinable* for *inclined*, that is, *disposed*. The endings *-ed* and *-able* or
-ible were often used interchangeably. See *Hamlet*, page 114, note 63.

We shall be blest to do,[5] if he remember
A kinder value of the people than
He hath hereto prized them at.

    Men.   That's off, that's off;[6]
I would you rather had been silent.   Please you
To hear Cominius speak?

    Bru.   Most willingly;
But yet my caution was more pertinent
Than the rebuke you give it.

    Men.   He loves your people;
But tie him not to be their bedfellow. —
Worthy Cominius, speak. — [CORIOLANUS *rises, and offers to*
      go away.] Nay, keep your place.

    1 Sen. Sit, Coriolanus; never shame to hear
What you have nobly done.

    Cor.   Your Honours' pardon:
I had rather have my wounds to heal again
Than hear say how I got them.

    Bru.   Sir, I hope
My words disbench'd you not.

    Cor.   No, sir; yet oft,
When blows have made me stay, I fled from words.
You soothed not,[7] therefore hurt not: but, your people,
I love them as they weigh.

    Men.   Pray now, sit down.

    Cor. I had rather have one scratch my head i' the sun,
When the alarum were struck, than idly sit
To hear my nothings monster'd.   [*Exit.*

---

   [5] *Blest to do* is no doubt the same as *blest,* that is, *happy, in doing.* The gerundial infinitive.

   [6] *From* the purpose, or *irrelevant;* hence Brutus declares it *pertinent.*

   [7] To *soothe* was sometimes used for to *flatter* or *cajole.*

Men.   Masters of the people,
Your multiplying spawn how can he flatter, —
That's thousand to one good one, — when you now see
He had rather venture all his limbs for honour
Than one on's ears to hear't? — Proceed, Cominius.

Com. I shall lack voice : the deeds of Coriolanus
Should not be utter'd feebly. — It is held
That valour is the chiefest virtue, and
Most dignifies the haver : if it be,
The man I speak of cannot in the world
Be singly counterpoised.   At sixteen years,
When Tarquin made a head[8] for Rome, he fought
Beyond the mark of others : our then Dictator,
Whom with all praise I point at, saw him fight,
When with his Amazonian chin he drove
The bristled lips before him : he bestrid
An o'er-press'd Roman,[9] and i' the Consul's view
Slew three opposers : Tarquin's self he met,
And struck him on his knee :[10] in that day's feats,
When he might act the woman in the scene,[11]
He proved best man i' the field, and for his meed
Was brow-bound with the oak.   His pupil-age
Man-enter'd thus, he waxèd like a sea ;
And, in the brunt of seventeen battles since,

[8] To *make a head* was in frequent use for to *raise* or to *lead an army*.

[9] To *bestride* a man when down upon the battle-field was considered an act of the greatest kindness ; and to save the life of a fellow-soldier in fight was one of the most honourable services a Roman could render to the State. See *Macbeth*, page 135, note 1.

[10] Not that he gave Tarquin a blow on the knee, but gave him such a blow as made him *fall on his knee*.

[11] In Shakespeare's time, women's parts were acted by *unbearded* youths, or by youngsters with " Amazonian chins."

He lurch'd all swords o' the garland.[12]   For this last,
Before and in Corioli, let me say,
I cannot speak him home : he stopp'd the fliers ;
And by his rare example made the coward
Turn terror into sport : as waves before
A vessel under sail, so men obey'd,
And fell below his stem : his sword, death's stamp,[13]
Where it did mark, it took ; from face to foot
He was a thing of blood, whose every motion
Was timed with dying cries : [14] alone he enter'd
The mortal gate o' the city, which he painted
With shunless destiny ; [15] aidless came off,
And with a sudden re-enforcement struck
Corioli like a planet.[16]   Now all's his :
When, by-and-by, the din of war 'gan pierce
His ready sense ; then straight his doubled spirit
Re-quicken'd what in flesh was fatigate,

[12] This use of *lurch* has occasioned a good deal of comment.   The best explanation of it that I have met with is in *The Edinburgh Review* for July, 1869 : "Both noun and verb were in use among the Elizabethan writers in the sense of *seizure*, *robbery*.   In the sense of engrossing, of seizing and carrying off with a high hand, *lurch* is also used amongst others by Bacon and Milton.   To *lurch* all swords of the garland, means therefore, not only to rob all swords of the garland, but to carry it away from them with an easy and victorious swoop."   The word, however, appears to have been only another spelling of *lurk ;* so that its radical sense is that of " going it on the sly " to *filch* or *steal.*

[13] The instrument with which Death *stamps* or *seals* men for his own.

[14] The cries of the dying *kept time with* every motion that he made.

[15] Stained with blood inevitably destined to flow where his sword was busy. — *Mortal* is *deadly* here, as it often is in old writers.

[16] This is well illustrated from *Timon of Athens*, iv. 3 :

> Be as a *planetary* plague, when Jove
> Will o'er some high-viced city hang his poison
> In the sick air : let not thy sword skip one.

And to the battle came he; where he did
Run reeking o'er the lives of men, as if
'Twere a perpetual spoil; and, till we call'd
Both field and city ours, he never stood
To ease his breast with panting.

   Men.   Worthy man!

   1 Sen. He cannot but with measure fit the honours
Which we devise him.

   Com.   Our spoils he kick'd at;
And look'd upon things precious as they were
The common muck o' the world: he covets less
Than misery [17] itself would give; rewards
His deeds with doing them; and is content
To spend the time to end it.[18]

   Men.   He's right noble:
Let him be call'd for.

   1 Sen.   Call Coriolanus.

   Off. He doth appear.

              Re-enter CORIOLANUS.

   Men. The Senate, Coriolanus, are well pleased
To make thee Consul.

   Cor.   I do owe them still
My life and services.

   Men.   It then remains
That you do speak to th' people.

   Cor.   I do beseech you,

---

[17] *Misery* for *avarice*, as *miser* signifies *avaricious*, or *miserly*.

[18] A strange expression; but probably meaning "content to end the time *in spending it*;" that is, loving valiant action for its own sake, regardless of any further considerations; and so not drawing upon the future or upon hope to sweeten his present service.

Let me o'erleap that custom ; for I cannot
Put on the gown, stand naked, and entreat them,
For my wounds' sake, to give their suffrage : please you
That I may pass this doing.

 Sic.   Sir, the people
Must have their voices; neither will they bate
One jot of ceremony.

 Men.   Put them not to't :
Pray you, go fit you to the custom ; and
Take to you, as your predecessors have,
Your honour with your form.[19]

 Cor.   It is a part
That I shall blush in acting, and might well
Be taken from the people.

 Bru. [*To* Sic.] Mark you that?

 Cor. To brag unto them, thus I did, and thus ;
Show them th' unaching scars which I should hide,
As if I had received them for the hire
Of their breath only ! —

 Men.   Do not stand upon't. —
We recommend to you, tribunes of the people,
Our purpose to them ;[20] and to our noble Consul
Wish we all joy and honour.

 Senators. To Coriolanus come all joy and honour !

   [*Flourish. Exeunt all but* BRUTUS *and* SICINIUS.

 Bru. You see how he intends to use the people.

 Sic. May they perceive's intent ! He will require them,

---

[19] "*Your* form " is the form which custom prescribes to you.

[20] Such is probably the right division of the line; though some have
printed it with the (;) after *purpose*, thus connecting *to them* with what
follows. But the last *to* is probably used for *towards* or *in reference to;*
" our purpose *towards* them."

As if he did contemn what he requested
Should be in them to give.[21]
    Bru.   Come, we'll inform them
Of our proceedings here : on th' market-place
I know they do attend[22] us.
                                       [*Exeunt.*

SCENE III. — *The Same.   The Forum.*

Enter several Citizens.

1 Cit. Once,[1] if he do require our voices, we ought not
to deny him.

2 Cit. We may, sir, if we will.

3 Cit. We have power in ourselves to do it, but it is a
power that we have no power to do :[2] for, if he show us his
wounds, and tell us his deeds, we are to put our tongues
into those wounds, and speak for them ; so, if he tell us
his noble deeds, we must also tell him our noble acceptance
of them.   Ingratitude is monstrous : and, for the multitude
to be ingrateful, were to make a monster of the multitude ;
of the which we being members, should bring ourselves to
be monstrous members.

---

[21] Contemn that it should be in their power to give that which he
requested.   This passage shows that *require* and *request* were used synony-
mously.   The Poet has many like instances.

[22] *Attend*, again, in the sense of *wait for*.   See page 73, note 7.

[1] *Once* was sometimes used in a way that is rather puzzling to us mod-
erns.   Here it seems to mean *enough*.   Staunton thinks it equivalent to
for the nonce ; but I cannot quite see that.   See *Much Ado*, p. 35, note 34.

[2] Power in the first instance here means *natural power*, or *force*, and then
moral power, or *right*.   Heath explains it thus : " We have indeed a power
by law to do it, if we think proper ; but this power amounts to the same as
no power at all, because we should offer the greatest violence to our very
natures, if we should exert it."

1 Cit. And to make us no better thought of, a little help will serve; for once we stood up about the corn, he himself stuck not to call us the many-headed multitude.

3 Cit. We have been called so of many; not that our heads are some brown, some black, some abram,[3] some bald, but that our wits are so diversely colour'd: and truly I think, if all our wits were to issue out of one skull, they would fly east, west, north, south; and their consent of one direct way should be at once to all the points o' the compass.

2 Cit. Think you so? Which way do you judge my wit would fly?

3 Cit. Nay, your wit will not so soon out as another man's will,—'tis strongly wedged up in a blockhead; but, if it were at liberty, 'twould, sure, southward.

2 Cit. Why that way?

3 Cit. To lose itself in a fog; where, being three parts melted away with rotten dews, the fourth would return for conscience sake, to help to get thee a wife.

2 Cit. You are never without your tricks: you may, you may.

3 Cit. Are you all resolved to give your voices? But that's no matter, the greater part carries it. I say, if he

---

[3] It appears that *abram* and *abraham* were used as epithets of colour, and that the particular colour designated by them was what we call *flaxen:* how or why they came to be so used, is involved in mystery. So in *Soliman and Perseda*, 1599: "Where is the eldest sonne of Pryam, that *abraham-colour'd* Trojon? dead." And in Middleton's *Blurt, Master Constable*, 1602: "A goodlie, long, thicke, *Abram-colour'd* beard." These passages do not indeed show *what* colour the terms meant; but Shakespeare elsewhere uses the phrase "*abram* Cupid"; and that ancient roguish imp of Venus was usually conceived and represented as *flaxen-haired.* Some, however, identify it with *auburn;* perhaps rightly. See *Romeo and Juliet*, page 67, note 3.

would incline to the people, there was never a worthier man.
Here he comes, and in the gown of humility : mark his behaviour. We are not to stay all together, but to come by
him where he stands, by ones, by twos, and by threes. He's
to make his requests by particulars ; wherein every one of
us has a single honour, in giving him our own voices with
our own tongues : therefore follow me, and I'll direct you
how you shall go by him.

    All. Content, content.   [*Exeunt.*

      Enter CORIOLANUS *and* MENENIUS.

    Men. O sir, you are not right : have you not known
The worthiest men have done't?
    Cor.   What must I say?
I pray, sir ; — Plague upon't ! I cannot bring
My tongue to such a pace ; — *look, sir; my wounds :*
I got them in my country's service, when
Some certain of your brethren roar'd, and ran
From th' noise of our own drums.
    Men.   O me, the gods !
You must not speak of that : you must desire them
To think upon you.
    Cor.   Think upon me ! hang 'em !
I would they would forget me, like the virtues
Which our divines lose by 'em.[4]
    Men.   You'll mar all :
I'll leave you : pray you, speak to 'em, I pray you,

---

[4] Probably, "the virtuous precepts which our divines lose their time in
preaching to them." — This use of the term *divines* has been set down as
another anachronism. No doubt it is so. And so in North's Plutarch we
often find that the ancient Greeks and Romans had *bishops* among them.
The Poet simply uses the language of his time to represent what has been
done at all times.

In wholesome [5] manner.

 Cor.   Bid them wash their faces,
And keep their teeth clean. [*Exit* MENENIUS.] — So, here
  comes a brace. —

Re-enter two Citizens.

You know the cause, sirs, of my standing here.

 1 Cit. We do, sir ; tell us what hath brought you to't.

 Cor. Mine own desert.

 2 Cit. Your own desert !

 Cor. Ay, not mine own desire.

 1 Cit. How ! not your own desire ?

 Cor. No, sir, 'twas never my desire yet to trouble the
poor with begging.

 1 Cit. You must think, if we give you any thing, we hope
to gain by you.

 Cor. Well, then, I pray, your price o' the consulship ?

 1 Cit. The price is, to ask it kindly.

 Cor. Kindly ! Sir, I pray, let me ha't : I have wounds
to show you, which shall be yours in private. — Your good
voice, sir ; what say you ?

 2 Cit. You shall ha't, worthy sir.

 Cor. A match, sir. — There's in all two worthy voices
begg'd. — I have your alms : adieu.

 1 Cit. But this is something odd.

 2 Cit. An 'twere to give again, — but 'tis no matter.

        [*Exeunt the two* Citizens.

Re-enter two other Citizens.

 Cor. Pray you now, if it may stand with the tune of your

---

5 *Wholesome* here plainly means *agreeable* or *pleasant.*

voices that I may be Consul, I have here the customary gown.

3 Cit. You have deserved nobly of your country, and you have not deserved nobly.

Cor. Your enigma?

3 Cit. You have been a scourge to her enemies, you have been a rod to her friends; you have not, indeed, loved the common people.

Cor. You should account me the more virtuous, that I have not been common in my love. I will, sir, flatter my sworn brother, the people, to earn a dearer estimation of them; 'tis a condition [6] they account gentle: and, since the wisdom of their choice is rather to have my hat than my heart, I will practise the insinuating nod, and be off to them [7] most counterfeitly; that is, sir, I will counterfeit the bewitchment of some popular man, and give it bountiful to the desirers. Therefore, beseech you I may be Consul.

4 Cit. We hope to find you our friend; and therefore give you our voices heartily.

3 Cit. You have received many wounds for your country.

Cor. I will not seal your knowledge [8] with showing them. I will make much of your voices, and so trouble you no further.

Both Cit. The gods give you joy, sir, heartily!

                                         [Exeunt.

Cor. Most sweet voices!—
Better it is to die, better to starve,
Than crave the hire which first we do deserve.

---

[6] *Condition*, as usual, for *disposition* or *temper*.

[7] That is, *off with my cap* to them. See page 86, note 2.

[8] "I will not strengthen or complete your knowledge." The *sealing* is that which finishes or ratifies a writing or contract.

Why in this woolvish toge [9] should I stand here,
To beg of Hob and Dick, that do appear,
Their needless vouches? [10]   Custom calls me to't.
What custom wills, in all things should we do't,
The dust on antique time would lie unswept,
And mountainous error be too highly heapt
For truth t' o'er-peer.   Rather than fool it so,
Let the high office and the honour go
To one that would do thus.   I am half through;
The one part suffer'd, th' other will I do.
Here come more voices. —

Re-enter three other Citizens.

Your voices : for your voices I have fought ;
Watch'd for your voices ; for your voices bear
Of wounds two dozen odd ; battles thrice six
I've seen and heard of ; [11] for your voices have

---

[9] *Toge* is a monosyllabic form of *toga*, the classical name of the civic *gown* which the Roman men wore in time of peace.   Here, of course, it is what was called the *toga candida*, which was worn by those who canvassed for an office, and who were thence termed *candidati*.   The *toga* was in fact made of wool; and an equivoque or double meaning was most likely intended in *woolvish*, referring both to the material of the gown and to the fact, that the speaker is in effect playing the part of a "wolf in sheep's clothing," wearing "the napless vesture of humility," while he is conscious of being any thing but humble within.

[10] He calls the "vouches" *needless*, because in his opinion an election by the Senate is or ought to be enough. — "*Hob* and *Dick*" are Roman roughs with rustic English names. — Mr. Joseph Crosby thinks *appear* is here used as a transitive verb, having *vouches* for its object, and meaning *show, offer*, or *present*.   It is indeed true that the Poet sometimes uses the word in that way : but here I think both sense and grammar come better if we take *vouches* as the object of *beg*.

[11] This, if the text be right, must mean, apparently, "I have taken part in eighteen battles, and those so considerable, that I have since heard them talked about."   See Critical Notes.

Done many things, some less, some more : your voices :
Indeed, I would be Consul.

5 Cit. He has done nobly, and cannot go without any
honest man's voice.

6 Cit. Therefore let him be Consul : the gods give him
joy, and make him good friend to the people !

All three Citizens. Amen, amen. — God save thee, noble
    Consul !   [*Exeunt.*

Cor. Worthy voices !

Re-enter MENENIUS, *with* BRUTUS *and* SICINIUS.

Men. You've stood your limitation ;[12] and the tribunes
Endue you with the people's voice : remains
That, in th' official marks invested, you
Anon do meet the Senate.

Cor.   Is this done ?

Sic. The custom of request you have discharged :
The people do admit you ; and are summon'd
To meet anon, upon your approbation.

Cor. Where ? at the Senate-house ?

Sic.   There, Coriolanus.

Cor. May I, then, change these garments ?

Sic.   You may, sir.

Cor. That I'll straight do ; and, knowing myself again,
Repair to th' Senate-house.

Men. I'll keep you company. — Will you along ?

Bru. We stay here for the people.

Sic.   Fare you well. —
        [*Exeunt* CORIOLANUS *and* MENENIUS.
He has it now ; and, by his looks, methinks

[12] " Your *limitation* " is your *appointment*, or *appointed time*. So the Poet
repeatedly uses to *limit* for to *appoint*. See *Macbeth*, page 88, note 34.

'Tis warm at's heart.

   Bru.   With a proud heart he wore
His humble weeds.   Will you dismiss the people?

Re-enter Citizens.

   Sic. How now, my masters! have you chose this man?

   1 Cit. He has our voices, sir.

   Bru. We pray the gods he may deserve your loves.

   2 Cit. Amen, sir.   To my poor unworthy notion,
He mock'd us when he begg'd our voices.

   3 Cit.   Certainly
He flouted us downright.

   1 Cit. No, 'tis his kind of speech; he did not mock us.

   2 Cit. Not one amongst us, save yourself, but says
He used us scornfully; he should have show'd us
His marks of merit, wounds received for's country.

   Sic. Why, so he did, I'm sure.

   All the Citizens.   No, no; no man saw 'em.

   3 Cit. He said he had wounds, which he could show in
       private;
And with his hat, thus waving it in scorn,
I would be Consul, says he; *agèd custom
But by your voices will not so permit me;
Your voices therefore.*   When we granted that,
Here was, *I thank you for your voices, — thank you, —
Your most sweet voices: now you've left your voices,
I have no further with you.*   Was not this mockery?

   Sic. Why either were you ignorant to see't,[13]
Or, seeing it, of such childish friendliness
To yield your voices?

---

13 " Why did you lack the sense to perceive it?"

Bru.　　　　　　　　Could you not have told him,
As you were lesson'd, when he had no power,
But was a petty servant to the State,
He was your enemy ; ever spake against
Your liberties, and the charters that you bear
I' the body of the weal ; and now, arriving
A place of potency,[14] and sway o' the State,
If he should still malignantly remain
Fast foe to th' plebeii, your voices might
Be curses to yourselves ?　 You should have said,
That as his worthy deeds did claim no less
Than what he stood for, so his gracious nature
Would think upon you for your voices, and
Translate his malice towards you into love,
Standing your friendly lord.
　　Sic.　　　　　　　　Thus to have said,
As you were fore-advised, had touch'd his spirit
And tried his inclination ; from him pluck'd
Either his gracious promise, which you might,
As cause had call'd you up, have held him to ;
Or else it would have gall'd his surly nature,
Which easily endures not article
Tying him to aught ; so, putting him to rage,
You should have ta'en th' advantage of his choler,
And pass'd him unelected.
　　Bru.　　　　　　　　Did you perceive
He did solicit you in free contempt,
When he did need your loves ; and do you think
That his contempt shall not be bruising to you,
When he hath power to crush ? 　Why, had your bodies

14 *Arrive* was sometimes used as a transitive verb. See *Julius Cæsar*, page 50, note 27.

No heart among you? or had you tongues to cry
Against the rectorship of judgment? [15]

   Sic.   Have you,
Ere now, denied the asker? and now again,
Of him [16] that did not ask, but mock, bestow
Your sued-for tongues?

   3 Cit.   He's not confirm'd; we may
Deny him yet.

   2 Cit.   And will deny him; I
Will have five hundred voices of that sound.

   1 Cit. I twice five hundred, and their friends to piece
      'em.

   Bru. Get you hence instantly; and tell those friends
They've chose a Consul that will from them take
Their liberties; make them of no more voice
Than dogs, that are as often beat for barking
As they are kept to do so.

   Sic.   Let them assemble;
And, on a safer judgment, all revoke
Your ignorant election: enforce [17] his pride,
And his old hate unto you: besides, forget not
With what contempt he wore the humble weed;
How in his suit he scorn'd you; but your loves,
Thinking upon his services, took from you
The apprehension of his present portance,[18]

---

[15] Tongues to *vote* otherwise than as your judgment *counselled* or *commanded*. *Rectorship* is *rule* or *government*.

[16] "*On* him," of course. The indiscriminate use of *on* and *of* occurs frequently. See *Romeo and Juliet*, page 36, note 5.

[17] *Enforce* in the sense of to *press* or *urge strongly*. So in iii. 3: "*Enforce* him with his envy to the people." And in *Julius Cæsar*, iii. 2: "Nor his offences *enforced*, for which he suffered death."

[18] *Portance* is *bearing* or *behaviour*. See *Othello*, page 68, note **13**.

Which, gibing most ungravely, he did fashion
After th' inveterate hate he bears you.

   Bru.   Lay
A fault on us, your tribunes ; that we labour'd
No impediment between, but that you must
Cast your election on him.[19]

   Sic.   Say you chose him
More after our commandment than as guided
By your own true affections ; and that your minds,
Pre-occupied with what you rather must do
Than what you should, made you against the grain
To voice him Consul : lay the fault on us.

   Bru. Ay, spare us not.   Say we read lectures to you,
How youngly he began to serve his country,
How long continued ; and what stock he springs of,
The noble House o' the Marcians ; from whence came
That Ancus Marcius, Numa's daughter's son,
Who, after great Hostilius, here was king ;
Of the same House Publius and Quintus were,
That our best water brought by conduits hither ;
And Censorinus, who was nobly named so,
Twice being chosen Censor by the people,
Was his great ancestor.

   Sic.   One thus descended,
That hath besides well in his person wrought
To be set high in place, we did commend

---

[19] The meaning seems to be, " we labour'd, or took pains, that there might
be no obstacle or hindrance, to excuse you from voting for him."   Endeav-
oured to have, or to leave, "no impediment between."   The language is
somewhat obscure. — Here we have a right piece of demagogical craft ;
the sneaking " wealsmen " trying to creep, underhand, into the good graces
of the patricians while setting the dogs to worrying them.

To your remembrances; but you have found,
Scaling his present bearing with his past,[20]
That he's your fixèd enemy, and revoke
Your sudden approbation.

   Bru.   Say you ne'er had done't —
Harp on that still — but by our putting on;[21]
And presently, when you have drawn your number,
Repair to th' Capitol.

   All the Citizens.   We will so: almost all
Repent in their election.[22]   [*Exeunt.*

   Bru.   Let them go on;
This mutiny were better put in hazard,
Than stay, past doubt, for greater:
If, as his nature is, he fall in rage
With their refusal, both observe and answer
The vantage of his anger.[23]

   Sic.   To th' Capitol, come:
We will be there before the stream o' the people;
And this shall seem, as partly 'tis, their own,
Which we have goaded onward.   [*Exeunt.*

---

  [20] Putting in the scales, that is, *weighing* or *balancing* his present conduct with his past.

  [21] *Putting on* in the sense of *instigating* or *inciting*. Often so.

  [22] Repent, that is, *change their mind, in regard to* the election, or *in the midst of* it. The election is not yet legally completed.

  [23] Be ready to take advantage of his anger: *meet the opportunity.*

ACT III.

Scene I. — *Rome.   A Street.*

Cornets.   Enter Coriolanus, Menenius, Cominius, Titus
Lartius, Senators, *and* Patricians.

Cor. Tullus Aufidius, then, had made new head?

Lart. He had, my lord; and that it was which caused
Our swifter composition.

Cor. So, then the Volsces stand but as at first;
Ready, when time shall prompt them, to make road
Upon's again.

Com.   They're worn, lord Consul, so,
That we shall hardly in our ages see
Their banners wave again.

Cor.   Saw you Aufidius?

Lart. On safe-guard[1] he came to me; and did curse
Against the Volsces, for they had so vilely
Yielded the town: he is retired to Antium.

Cor. Spoke he of me?

Lart.   He did, my lord.

Cor.   How? what?

Lart. How often he had met you, sword to sword;
That of all things upon the Earth he hated
Your person most; that he would pawn his fortunes
To hopeless restitution,[2] so he might
Be call'd your vanquisher.

---

[1] *On safe-guard* is, with a guard to protect him.

[2] "To hopeless restitution" means beyond the hope of restitution or
recovery.   Shakespeare has many like forms of expression.

Cor.   At Antium lives he?

Lart. At Antium.

Cor. I wish I had a cause to seek him there,
T' oppose his hatred fully.   Welcome home. —

Enter SICINIUS *and* BRUTUS.

Behold, these are the tribunes of the people,
The tongues o' the common mouth : I do despise them :
For they do prank them in authority,
Against all noble sufferance.

Sic.   Pass no further.

Cor. Ha ! what is that?

Bru. It will be dangerous to go on : no further.

Cor. What makes this change?

Men. The matter?

Com. Hath he not pass'd the nobles and the commons?

Bru. Cominius, no.

Cor.   Have I had children's voices?

1 Sen. Tribunes, give way ; he shall to th' market-place.

Bru. The people are incensed against him.

Sic.   Stop,
Or all will fall in broil.

Cor.   Are these your herd?
Must these have voices, that can yield them now,
And straight disclaim their tongues?   What are your offices?
You being their mouths, why rule you not their teeth?
Have you not set them on?

Men.   Be calm, be calm.

Cor. It is a purposed thing, and grows by plot,
To curb the will of the nobility :
Suffer't, and live with such as cannot rule,

Nor ever will be ruled.

Bru.   Call't not a plot :

The people cry you mock'd them ; and of late,

When corn was given them gratis, you repined ;

Scandal'd the suppliants for the people ; call'd them

Time-pleasers, flatterers, foes to nobleness.

Cor. Why, this was known before.

Bru.   Not to them all.

Cor. Have you inform'd them sithence ? [3]

Bru.   How ! I inform them !

Cor. You're like to do such business.

Bru.   Not unlike,

Each way, to better yours. [4]

Cor. Why, then, should I be Consul ?   By yond clouds,

Let me deserve so ill as you, and make me

Your fellow tribune.

Sic.   You show too much of that

For which the people stir : if you will pass

To where you're bound, you must inquire your way,

Which you are out of, with a gentler spirit ;

Or never be so noble as a Consul,

Nor yoke with him for tribune.

Men.   Let's be calm.

Com. The people are abused ; set on.   This paltering [5]

---

[3] *Sithence* and *sith* are old forms of the temporal and causal *since*.   Both were lapsing out of use in Shakespeare's time, and *since* was replacing them ; but he has *sith* repeatedly, and *sithence* in one other place.   Hooker uses *sith* and *sithence* a great deal ; *since*, very little.

[4] That is, not unlikely to better, to *surpass*, your doing, or your action, in *every* way.   To which the reply is pertinent, "Why, then, should I be Consul ?"   The use of to *better* for to *surpass* occurs repeatedly.   See vol. vii. page 216, note 19.

[5] *Paltering* is *shuffling*, *dodging*, *haggling*, or *playing fast and loose*.   See *Macbeth*, page 164, note 5.

Becomes not Rome ; nor has Coriolanus
Deserved this so dishonour'd rub, laid falsely
I' the plain way of his merit.[6]

 Cor.   Tell me of corn !
This was my speech, and I will speak't again, —

 Men. Not now, not now.

 1 Sen.   Not in this heat, sir, now.

 Cor. Now, as I live, I will. My nobler friends,
I crave their pardons :
For th' mutable, rank-scented many, let them
Regard me as I do not flatter, and
Therein behold themselves.[7] I say again,
In soothing[8] them, we nourish 'gainst our Senate
The cockle[9] of rebellion, insolence, sedition,
Which we ourselves have plough'd for, sow'd, and scatter'd,
By mingling them with us, the honour'd number ;
Who lack not virtue, no, nor power, but that
Which they have given to beggars.

 Men.   Well, no more.

 1 Sen. No more words, we beseech you.

 Cor.   How ! no more !
As for my country I have shed my blood,

---

 [6] An allusion to bowling; a *rub* being a *hindrance, impediment*, or any thing that deflects the bowl from its aim. — *Falsely* is *treacherously.* — *Dishonour'd* for *dishonouring*, or *dishonourable*, either of which senses fits the context, while both are in accordance with old usage.

 [7] " Let them regard this in me, that I am no flatterer, but speak my honest thought ; and let them see themselves as they are, in the glass of my plain, unflattering speech."

 [8] *Soothing* is *flattering, indulging, feeding their humour.*

 [9] *Cockle* is a weed which grows up and chokes the corn. The thought is from North's Plutarch : " Moreover, he said that they nourished against themselves the naughty seed and *cockle* of insolency and sedition, which had been sowed and scattered abroad among the people."

Not fearing outward force, so shall my lungs
Coin words till their decay against those measles,[10]
Which we disdain should tetter us, yet sought
The very way to catch them.

  Bru.   You speak o' the people,
As if you were a god to punish, not
A man of their infirmity.

  Sic.   'Twere well
We let the people know't.

  Men.   What, what? his choler?

  Cor. Choler!
Were I as patient as the midnight sleep,
By Jove, 'twould be my mind!

  Sic.   It is a mind
That shall remain a poison where it is,
Not poison any further.

  Cor.   *Shall remain!* —
Hear you this Triton of the minnows? mark you
His absolute *shall?*

  Com.   'Twas from the canon.[11]

  Cor.   *Shall!*
O good, but most unwise patricians! why,
You grave, but reckless Senators, have you thus
Given Hydra here[12] to choose an officer,
That with his peremptory *shall,* being but
The horn and noise o' the monster,[13] wants not spirit

---

[10] *Meazel,* or *mesell,* is an old term for a *leper.*

[11] That is, 'twas out of order, *diverse from the rule* of legal right.

[12] *Hydra* is what the same speaker afterwards describes as "the beast with many heads." — *Given* is here equivalent to *allowed* or *empowered:* given them the prerogative of choosing. See Critical Notes.

[13] The horn through which the beast aforesaid trumpets forth his noise.

To say he'll turn your current in a ditch,
And make your channel his?   If they have power,
Let them have cushions by you; if none, revoke
Your dangerous lenity.   If you are learned,
Be not as common fools; if you are not,
Then vail [14] your ignorance.   You are plebeians,
If they be Senators: and they are no less,
When, both your voices blended, the great'st taste
Most palates theirs.[15]   They choose their magistrate;
And such a one as he, who puts his *shall*,
His popular *shall*, against a graver bench
Than ever frown'd in Greece.   By Jove himself,
It makes the Consuls base! and my soul aches
To know, when two authorities are up,
Neither supreme, how soon confusion
May enter 'twixt the gap of both, and take
The one by th' other.
 Com.   Well; on to th' market-place.
 Cor.   Whoever gave that counsel, to give forth
The corn o' the storehouse gratis, as 'twas used
Sometime in Greece, —
 Men.   Well, well, no more of that.
 Cor.   —Though there the people had more absolute
   power, —
I say, they nourish'd disobedience, fed

---

[14] To *vail* is to *lower*, to *let fall*, to *abase*.   See *Hamlet*, page 59, note 20.

[15] To *palate* is commonly used with reference to the sense or organ of taste; here, with reference to the thing tasted, or the flavour that affects the palate.   I quote Mr. R. Whitelaw's happy explanation of the passage: "'The prevailing flavour of the whole smacks rather of their voice than of yours.'   Judged by results, — the taste it leaves in the mouth, — this dualized government of compromise gives expression to the popular, rather than to the patrician, will: the tribunicial *nay* is stronger than the consular *yea*."

The ruin of the State.

Bru.   Why, shall the people give
One, that speaks thus, their voice?

Cor.   I'll give my reasons,
More worthier than their voices.   They know the corn
Was not our recompense,[16] resting well assured
They ne'er did service for't.   Being press'd to th' war,
Even when the navel of the State was touch'd,
They would not thread the gates : [17] this kind of service
Did not deserve corn gratis.   Being i' the war,
Their mutinies and revolts, wherein they show'd
Most valour, spoke not for them.   Th' accusation
Which they have often made against the Senate,
All cause unborn, could never be the motive
Of our so frank donation.   Well, what then?
How shall this bisson multitude digest
The Senate's courtesy?   Let deeds express
What's like to be their words : [18] *We did request it;*
We are the greater poll,[19] *and in true fear*
They gave us our demands.   Thus we debase
The nature of our seats, and make the rabble
Call our cares fears ; which will in time break ope

[16] " *Our recompense* " would now mean the recompense *received* by us;
here it means the recompense *given* by us; *our* being what is called the
subjective genitive; that is, having reference to the *subject* or source, and
not to the *object* or recipient, of the recompense.   In Shakespeare's time,
the objective and subjective genitives were often used indiscriminately,
where such use is now obsolete.   See *The Tempest*, page 138, note 23.

[17] To " *thread* the gates " is to pass through them.   So in *King Richard
the Second*, v. 5 : " To *thread* the *postern* of a small neeld's eye."

[18] " Let their past deeds be taken as an indication of what they are likely
to speak openly."

[19] *Poll* was used for *head :* here it is *number ;* as to *poll* is to *count by
the head.*

The locks o' the Senate, and bring in the crows
To peck the eagles.

   Men.   Come, enough.

   Bru. Enough, with over-measure.

   Cor.   No, take more :
What may be sworn by, both divine and human,
Seal what I end withal !   This double worship, —
Where one part does disdain with cause, the other
Insult without all reason ; where gentry, title, wisdom,
Cannot conclude but by the yea and no
Of general ignorance, — it must omit
Real necessities, and give way the while
T' unstable slightness : purpose so barr'd, it follows,
Nothing is done to purpose.   Therefore, beseech you, —
You that will be less fearful than discreet ;
That love the fundamental part of State
More than you doubt [20] the change on't ; that prefer
A noble life before a long, and wish
To jump [21] a body with a dangerous physic
That's sure of death without it, — at once pluck out
The multitudinous tongue ; let them not lick
The sweet which is their poison : your dishonour
Mangles true judgment,[22] and bereaves the State
Of that integrity which should become't ;
Not having the power to do the good it would,
For th' ill which doth control't.

   [20] Here, as in many other places, *doubt* is equivalent to *fear*.

   [21] To *jump* is to *risk* or *hazard ;* referring to the kill-or-cure treatment that is sometimes resorted to in desperate cases. — The " dangerous physic" which Coriolanus contemplates is the abolition of the tribunate ; and he does not shirk the likelihood, that this will cause an earthquake in the State.

   [22] "The dishonour heaped upon you hacks and maims the august form of Justice." — *Integrity*, in the next line, is *unity of purpose*.   A Latinism.

Bru.   'Has said enough.

Sic. 'Has spoken like a traitor, and shall answer
As traitors do.

Cor.   Thou wretch, despite o'erwhelm thee !—
What should the people do with these bald [23] tribunes?
On whom depending, their obedience fails
To th' greater bench : in a rebellion,
When what's not meet, but what must be, was law,
Then were they chosen : in a better hour,
Let what is meet be said it must be meet,
And throw their power i' the dust. [24]

Bru. Manifest treason !

Sic.   This a Consul? no.

Bru. Th' ædiles, ho !

*Enter an Æ*dile.

Let him be apprehended.

Sic. Go, call the people ; [*Exit* Ædile.] — in whose name myself
Attach thee as a traitorous innovator,
A foe to th' public weal : obey, I charge thee,
And follow to thine answer.

Cor.   Hence, old goat !

Sen. ⎫
Pat. ⎭ We'll surety him.

Com. Agèd sir, hands off.

Cor. Hence, rotten thing ! or I shall shake thy bones
Out of thy garments.

---

[23] *Bald* is, properly, *naked, bare ;* hence *empty, senseless ;* as in *balderdash.* So in *1 Henry IV.,* i. 3 : "This *bald,* unjointed chat of his."

[24] "Let it be said by you that what is meet to be done, *must* be meet, that is, *shall be done,* and put an end at once to the tribunitian power."

Sic.   Help, ye citizens !

Enter a Rabble of Citizens, *with the* Ædiles.

Men. On both sides more respect.

Sic. Here's he that would take from you all your power.

Bru. Seize him, ædiles !

Citizens. Down with him ! down with him !

Sen. ⎫
Pat. ⎬ Weapons, weapons, weapons ! —
&c. ⎭
                        [*They all bustle about* CORIOLANUS.

Tribunes ! — Patricians ! — Citizens ! — What, ho ! —
Sicinius ! — Brutus ! — Coriolanus ! — Citizens ! —
Peace, peace, peace ! — Stay, hold, peace !

Men. What is about to be ? I'm out of breath ;
Confusion's near ; I cannot speak. — You, tribunes,
Speak to the people ; — Coriolanus, patience ; —
Speak, good Sicinius.

Sic.   Hear me, people ; peace !

Citizens. Let's hear our tribune : peace ! — Speak, speak,
        speak.

Sic. You are at point to lose your liberties :
Marcius would have all from you ; Marcius,
Whom late you've named for Consul.

Men.   Fie, fie, fie !
This is the way to kindle, not to quench.

1 Sen. T' unbuild the city, and to lay all flat.

Sic. What is the city but the people ?

Citizens.   True,
The people are the city.

Bru. By the consent of all, we were establish'd
The people's magistrates.

Citizens.   **You** so remain.

Men. And so are like to do.

Cor. That is the way to lay the city flat ; 25
To bring the roof to the foundation,
And bury all, which yet distinctly ranges,
In heaps and piles of ruin.

Sic. This deserves death.

Bru. Or let us stand to our authority,
Or let us lose it. — We do here pronounce,
Upon the part o' the people, in whose power
We were elected theirs, Marcius is worthy
Of present death.

Sic. Therefore lay hold of him ;
Bear him to th' rock Tarpeian, and from thence
Into destruction cast him.

Bru. Ædiles, seize him !

Citizens. Yield, Marcius, yield !

Men. Hear me one word :
Beseech you, tribunes, hear me but a word.

Æd. Peace, peace !

Men. Be that you seem, truly your country's friends,
And temperately proceed to what you would
Thus violently redress.

Bru. Sir, those cold ways,
That seem like prudent helps, are very poisonous
Where the disease is violent. — Lay hands upon him,
And bear him to the rock.

Cor. [*Drawing his sword.*] No, I'll die here.
There's some among you have beheld me fighting :
Come, try upon yourselves what you have seen me.

---

25 Meaning, no doubt, that retaining the Tribunes in power is " the way
to lay the city flat," &c. The Tribunes naturally regard this as a treasonable
assertion.

Men. Down with that sword !—Tribunes, withdraw awhile.

Bru. Lay hands upon him.

Men.   Help, help Marcius, help,

You that be noble ; help him, young and old !

Citizens. Down with him ! down with him !

> [*In this mutiny the* Tribunes, *the* Ædiles,
> *and the* People *are beat in.*

Men. Go, get you to your house ; be gone, away !

All will be naught else.

2 Sen.   Get you gone.

Cor.   Stand fast ;

We have as many friends as enemies.

Men. Shall it be put to that?

1 Sen.   The gods forbid !—

I pr'ythee, noble friend, home to thy house ;

Leave us to cure this cause.

Men.   For 'tis a sore upon us,

You cannot tent yourself : be gone, beseech you.

Com. Come, sir, along with us.

Cor. I would they were barbarians, as they are,

Though in Rome litter'd ; not Romans, as they are not,

Though calved i' the porch o' the Capitol, —

Men.   Be gone ;

Put not your worthy rage into your tongue ;

One time will owe another.[26]

Cor.   On fair ground

I could beat forty of them.

Men. I could myself take up a brace o' the best

Of them ; yea, the two tribunes.

---

26 "Our turn of success will come." Or, "another time will recompense
us for the defeat and dishonour of to-day."

Com. But now 'tis odds beyond arithmetic ;
And manhood is call'd foolery, when it stands
Against a falling fabric. — Will you hence,
Before the tag return ? whose rage doth rend
Like interrupted waters, and o'erbear
What they are used to bear.

Men.   Pray you, be gone :
I'll try whether my old wit be in request
With those that have but little : this must be patch'd
With cloth of any colour.

Com.   Nay, come away.

[*Exeunt* CORIOLANUS, COMINIUS, *and others.*

1 Pat. This man has marr'd his fortune.

Men. His nature is too noble for the world :
He would not flatter Neptune for his trident,
Or Jove for's power to thunder.   His heart's his mouth :
What his breast forges, that his tongue must vent ;
And, being angry, does forget that ever
He heard the name of death. [*A noise within.*] Here's
    goodly work !

2 Pat. I would they were a-bed !

Men. I would they were in Tiber ! What, the vengeance,
Could he not speak 'em fair ?

Re-enter BRUTUS *and* SICINIUS, *with the Rabble.*

Sic.   Where is this viper,
That would depopulate the city, and
Be every man himself ?

Men.   You worthy tribunes, —

Sic. He shall be thrown down the Tarpeian rock
With rigorous hands ; he hath resisted law,
And therefore law shall scorn him further trial

Than the severity of the public power,
Which he so sets at nought.

1 Cit.   He shall well know
The noble tribunes are the people's mouths,
And we their hands.

Citizens.   He shall, sure on't.

Men.   Sir, sir, —

Sic. Peace !

Men. Do not cry havoc,[27] where you should but hunt
With modest warrant.

Sic.   Sir, how comes't that you
Have holp to make this rescue?

Men.   Hear me speak :
As I do know the Consul's worthiness,
So can I name his faults, —

Sic.   Consul ! what Consul?

Men. The Consul Coriolanus.

Bru. He Consul !

Citizens. No, no, no, no, no.

Men. If, by the tribunes' leave, and yours, good people,
I may be heard, I'd crave a word or two ;
The which shall turn you to no further harm
Than so much loss of time.

Sic.   Speak briefly, then ;
For we are peremptory to dispatch
This viperous traitor : to eject him hence
Were but our danger ; and to keep him here
Our certain death : therefore it is decreed
He dies to-night.

---

[27] *Havoc* was the signal for giving no quarter in battle ; and any one who
should " cry *havoc*," without authority from the commanding general, was to
be punished with death. See *Julius Cæsar*, page 115, note 43.

Men.   Now the good gods forbid
That our renownèd Rome, whose gratitude
Towards her deservèd [28] children is enroll'd
In Jove's own book, like an unnatural dam
Should now eat up her own !

Sic. He's a disease that must be cut away.

Men. O, he's a limb that has but a disease ;
Mortal, to cut it off ; to cure it, easy.
What has he done to Rome that's worthy death ?
Killing our enemies, the blood he hath lost —
Which, I dare vouch, is more than that he hath,
By many an ounce — he dropp'd it for his country ;
And what is left, to lose it by his country,
Were to us all, that do't and suffer it,
A brand to th' end o' the world.

Sic.   This is clean kam.[29]

Bru. Merely [30] awry : when he did love his country,
It honour'd him.

Men.   The service of the foot
Being once gangrened, is not then respected
For what before it was.[31]

Bru.   We'll hear no more. —

---

[28] *Deserved* for *deserving ;* an instance of the indiscriminate use of active and passive forms so common in Shakespeare. I have noted many such cases. See *King Lear*, page 67, note 49.

[29] *All wrong ;* the same as " merely awry " in the next line. *Kam* is an old word for *crooked ;* thus explained by Cotgrave : " All goes cleane contrarie, quite *kamme*." *Clean kam* appears to have been corrupted into *kimkam ;* of which word Holland's Plutarch furnishes several instances : " First mark, I beseech you, the comparison, how they go clean *kim-kam*, and against the stream, as if rivers run up hills."

[30] *Merely*, here, is *utterly* or *absolutely.* Often so.

[31] Here Menenius is probably to be understood as urging the logical consequences of the Tribune's position, by way of refuting it.

Pursue him to his house, and pluck him thence ;
Lest his infection, being of catching nature,
Spread further.
    Men.   One word more, one word.
This tiger-footed rage, when it shall find
The harm of unscann'd [32] swiftness, will, too late,
Tie leaden pounds to's heels.   Proceed by process ;
Lest parties — as he is beloved — break out,
And sack great Rome with Romans.
    Bru.   If't were so, —
    Sic. What do ye talk?
Have we not had a taste of his obedience?
Our ædiles smote? [33] ourselves resisted? — Come, —
    Men. Consider this : He has been bred i' the wars
Since he could draw a sword, and is ill school'd
In bolted language ; meal and bran together
He throws without distinction.   Give me leave,
I'll go to him, and undertake to bring him
Where he shall answer, by a lawful form, —
In peace, — to's utmost peril.
    1 Sen.   Noble tribunes,
It is the húmane way : the other course
Will prove too bloody ; and the end of it
Unknown to the beginnning.
    Sic.   Noble Menenius,
Be you, then, as the people's officer. —
Masters, lay down your weapons.
    Bru.   Go not home.

---

[32] *Unscann'd* here means *heedless, inconsiderate, rash.*

[33] The writers of Shakespeare's time did not much mind the classical pronunciation of Greek and Latin names. So, here. *Ædiles* is used as a word of two syllables.   The same once, if not twice, before in this scene.

Sic. Meet on the market-place. — We'll attend you there ;
Where, if you bring not Marcius, we'll proceed
In our first way.

Men. I'll bring him to you. — [*To the* Senators.] Let me
Desire your company : he must come, or what
Is worst will follow.

1 Sen.   Pray you, let us to him.   [*Exeunt*

SCENE II. — *A Room in* CORIOLANUS'S *House.*

Enter CORIOLANUS *and* Patricians.

Cor. Let them pull all about mine ears ; present me
Death on the wheel or at wild horses' heels ;
Or pile ten hills on the Tarpeian rock,
That the precipitation might down stretch
Below the beam of sight ; yet will I still
Be thus to them.

1 Pat.   You do the nobler.

Cor. I muse [1] my mother
Does not approve me further, who was wont
To call them woollen vassals,[2] things created
To buy and sell with groats ; to show bare heads
In congregations ; to yawn, be still, and wonder,
When one but of my ordinance [3] stood up
To speak of peace or war. —

Enter VOLUMNIA.

I talk of you :

---

[1] *Muse* for *wonder ;* a frequent usage.   See *Macbeth*, page 114, note 12.

[2] That is, wretches, or loafers, unfit for war, and good for nothing but to
wear the cowardly toga.   See page 98, note 9.

[3] *Ordinance* is here used, apparently, for *order* or *rank*.

Why did you wish me milder? would you have me
False to my nature?   Rather say, I play
Truly the man I am.

    Vol.   O, sir, sir, sir,[4]
I would have had you put your power well on,
Before you had worn it out.

    Cor.   Let go.

    Vol. You might have been enough the man you are,
With striving less to be so : lesser had been
The thwartings of your disposition, if
You had not show'd them how ye were disposed
Ere they lack'd power to cross you.

    Cor.   Let them hang.

    Vol. Ay, and burn too.

            Enter MENENIUS *and* Senators.

    Men. Come, come, you've been too rough, something too
       rough ;
You must return and mend it.

    1 Sen.   There's no remedy ;
Unless, by not so doing, our good city
Cleave in the midst, and perish.

    Vol.   Pray, be counsell'd :
I have a heart as tickle-apt [5] as yours,

---

   [4] Dyce aptly suggests that the use of *sir, sir, sir* may be meant as a mild,
but significant note of displeasure at the hero's conduct: "one of Shakespeare's touches of nature."

   [5] As dangerous to meddle with; as sensitive; as apt to explode if stirred,
or to fire up if touched with provocation. The Poet has *tickle* repeatedly
in a kindred sense. See *Hamlet*, page 109, note 44. So in North's Plutarch : "Some men feared lest he would bring all the city in an uproar,
considering it stood then but in very *tickle* terms." And in Fletcher's *Rule
a Wife and have a Wife*, iii. 1: "Courtiers are but *tickle* things to deal
withal." Also in Holland's Pliny : "For who knoweth not, that in frost it is

But yet a brain that leads my use of anger
To better vantage.

   Men.   Well said, noble woman !
Before he should thus stoop to th' herd, but that
The violent fit o' the time craves it as physic
For the whole State, I'd put mine armour on,
Which I can scarcely bear.

   Cor.   What must I do?

   Men. Return to th' tribunes.

   Cor.   Well, what then? what then?

   Men. Repent what you have spoke.

   Cor. For them? I cannot do it to the gods ;
Must I, then, do't to them?

   Vol.   You are too absolute ;
Though therein you can never be too noble,
But when extremities speak. I've heard you say,
Honour and policy, like unsever'd friends,
I' the war do grow together : grant that, and tell me,
In peace what each of them by th' other lose,
That they combine not there.

   Cor.   Tush, tush !

   Men.   A good demand.

---

ticklish medling with vines, and that they be in daunger soone to breake
and knap asunder." Still more to the purpose is a passage in Chapman's
Byron's Conspiracy, 1608 :

> Colonel Williams,
> A worthy captain, would compare with him,
> And hold his swelling valor to the mark ;
> And, as in open vessels fill'd with water,
> And on men's shoulders borne, they put treen cups,
> To keep the wild and slippery element
> From washing over ; follow all his sways
> And *tickle-aptness to exceed his bounds,*
> And in the brim contain him.

Vol. If it be honour in your wars to seem
The same you are not, — which, for your best ends,
You adopt your policy, — how is it less or worse,
That it shall hold companionship in peace
With honour, as in war ; since that to both
It stands in like request?

    Cor.   Why force you this?

    Vol. Because that now it lies you on [6] to speak
To th' people ; not by your own instruction,
Nor by the matter which your own heart prompts you,
But with such words that are but roted in
Your tongue, thought's bastards, and but syllables
Of no allowance to your bosom's truth.[7]
Now, this no more dishonours you at all
Than to take-in [8] a town with gentle words,
Which else would put you to your fortune, and
The hazard of much blood.
I would dissemble with my nature, where
My fortunes and my friends at stake required

---

[6] "It lies you on," or "it stands you on," is an old phrase for "it is *incumbent* on you," or "it is your part and duty." See *Hamlet*, p. 216, n. 15.

[7] *Allowance* is here used in the old sense of to *allow*, that is, to *justify* or *approve ;* as in Psalm xi. of the Psalter : "The Lord *alloweth* the righteous." Also in many other places of the English Bible. Shakespeare has *allowance* repeatedly in the same sense ; as in *King Lear*, i. 4 : "That you protect this course, and put it on by your *allowance*." — The best explanation of the passage in the text, that I have met with, is furnished me by Mr. Joseph Crosby : "Truth sits enthroned on your bosom, to sanction your thoughts and language : but, in the present case, your words will be but illegitimate offspring, not born of your heart, having no approval or justification from that truth ; but merely roted in your *tongue*, — spoken, as a parrot or child talks, *by rote*." A verse from Psalm cxxxix., of the Psalter, is not irrelevant here : "There is not a *word in my tongue*, but Thou, O Lord, knowest it altogether."

[8] *Take-in*, again, in the sense of *capture* or *subdue*. See page 51, note 5.

I should do so in honour : I am in this,
Your wife, your son,[9] these Senators, the nobles ;
And you will rather show our general louts
How you can frown than spend a fawn upon 'em,
For the inheritance of their loves, and safeguard
Of what that want [10] might ruin.

    Men.   Noble lady ! —
Come, go with us ; speak fair : you may salve so,
Not [11] what is dangerous present, but the loss
Of what is past.

    Vol.   I pr'ythee now, my son,
Go to them, with this bonnet in thy hand ;
And — thus far having stretch'd it, (here be with them,)
Thy knee bussing the stones, (for in such business
Action is eloquence, and th' eyes of th' ignorant
More learnèd than the ears,) waving thy head,
Which often, thus, correcting thy stout heart,
Bow, humble as the ripest mulberry
That will not hold the handling — say to them,
Thou art their soldier, and, being bred in broils,
Hast not the soft way which, thou dost confess,
Were fit for thee to use, as they to claim,
In asking their good loves ; but thou wilt frame
Thyself, forsooth, hereafter theirs, so far
As thou hast power and person.

    Men.   This but done,
Even as she speaks it, why, their hearts were yours ;

---

[9] Meaning, apparently, " I am in, or *of*, this *mind ; so is* your wife, your son," &c.   Or the sense may be, " I am, in this, your wife " ; that is, " in this advice I express the thought of your wife," &c.

[10] *That want* is *the want of that*, namely, " their loves."

[11] *Not* is here equivalent to *not only.*

For they have pardons, being ask'd, as free
As words to little purpose.
   Vol.   Pr'ythee now,
Go, and be ruled : although I know thou hadst rather
Follow thine enemy in [12] a fiery gulf
Than flatter him in a bower.   Here is Cominius.

Enter COMINIUS.

   Com. I've been i' the market-place ; and, sir, 'tis fit
You make strong party, or defend yourself
By calmness or by absence : all's in anger.
   Men. Only fair speech.
   Com.   I think 'twill serve, if he
Can thereto frame his spirit.
   Vol.   He must, and will. —
Pr'ythee now, say you will, and go about it.
   Cor. Must I go show them my unbarbèd sconce? [13]
Must I with my base tongue give to my heart
A lie that it must bear?   Well, I will do't:

---

[12] Here, again, *in* has the sense of *into*.   See page 49, note 1.

[13] The Poet repeatedly uses *sconce* for *head*. — *Unbarbed* is explained by
Dyce and some others as *unshorn, untrimmed ;* which can hardly be right,
as the speech clearly refers, not to personal appearance, but to the customary
signs of deference and humility, one of which was standing bare-headed,
and bowing in a lowly manner to the assembled citizens.   And so *The
Edinburgh Review* for October, 1872, shows conclusively, in a passage too
long for quotation here, that *barbe* was often used for any head-covering ;
the writer adding that "to show an unbarbed sconce is to show an un-
covered, unprotected sconce ; in other words, to appear bare-headed."   This
accords with what Volumnia has just said to her son : "Go to them, with
this *bonnet in thy hand.*" — In the next line, "my *base* tongue" is a clear
instance of prolepsis ; meaning tongue *that will be* base, if he uses it in
the way proposed.   The Poet has a good many such proleptical forms of
speech.   See *2 Henry IV.*, page 170, note 1.

Yet, were there but this single plot [14] to lose,
This mould of Marcius, they to dust should grind it,
And throw't against the wind. — To th' market-place! —
You've put me now to such a part, which never
I shall discharge to th' life.

   Com.   Come, come, we'll prompt you.

   Vol. I pr'ythee now, sweet son, as thou hast said
My praises made thee first a soldier, so,
To have my praise for this, perform a part
Thou hast not done before.

   Cor.   Well, I must do't:
Away my disposition, and possess me
Some harlot's spirit! my throat of war be turn'd,
Which quirèd with my drum,[15] into a pipe
Small as an eunuch's, or the virgin voice
That babies lulls asleep![16] the smiles of knaves
Tent in my cheeks; and schoolboys' tears take up
The glasses of my sight! a beggar's tongue
Make motion through my lips; and my arm'd knees,
Who bow'd but in my stirrup, bend like his
That hath received an alms! — I will not do't;
Lest I surcease to honour mine own truth,
And by my body's action teach my mind
A most inherent baseness.

   Vol.   At thy choice, then:

---

  14 *Plot* is piece, portion, applied to a piece of earth, and here transferred to the body.

  15 Which *played in concert* with my drum. So in *The Merchant of Venice:* " Still *quiring* to the young-eyed cherubins."

  16 White notes *virgin* here as an " infelicitous use of epithet." I cannot conceive why, unless on the ground that virgins never use their voice in singing lullaby to other people's children. Do none but mothers lull babies asleep?

To beg of thee, it is my more dishonour
Than thou of them.   Come all to ruin : let
Thy mother rather feel thy pride than fear
Thy dangerous stoutness ; [17] for I mock at death
With as big heart as thou.   Do as thou list.
Thy valiantness was mine, thou suck'dst it from me ;
But owest thy pride thyself.

 Cor.   Pray, be content :
Mother, I'm going to the market-place ;
Chide me no more.   I'll mountebank their loves,
Cog [18] their hearts from them, and come home beloved
Of all the trades in Rome.   Look, I am going :
Commend me to my wife.   I'll return Consul ;
Or never trust to what my tongue can do
I' the way of flattery further.

 Vol.   Do your will.   [*Exit.*

 Com. Away ! the tribunes do attend you : [19] arm yourself
To answer mildly ; for they are prepared
With accusations, as I hear, more strong
Than are upon you yet.

 Cor. The word is *mildly.* — Pray you, let us go :
Let them accuse me by invention, I
Will answer in mine honour.

 Men.   Ay, but mildly.

 Cor. Well, mildly be it, then ; mildly !   [*Exeunt.*

---

[17] The meaning probably is, "let me suffer the worst that thy pride can bring upon me, rather than thus live in fear of what will grow from thy obstinacy."

[18] To *mountebank* is, here, to *play the conjurer.* — To *cog* is to *cheat,* to *wheedle,* to *lie.* See *Much Ado,* page 109, note 8.

[19] Here, again, *attend* is *wait for* or *await.* See page 73, note 7.

SCENE III. — *Same. The Forum.*

Enter SICINIUS *and* BRUTUS.

Bru. In this point charge him home, that he affects
Tyrannical power: if he evade us there,
Enforce him with his envy [1] to the people;
And that the spoil got on the Antiates
Was ne'er distributed. —

Enter an Ædile.

What, will he come?
    Æd.   He's coming.
    Bru.   How accompanied?
    Æd. With old Menenius, and those Senators
That always favour'd him.
    Sic.   Have you a catalogue
Of all the voices that we have procured,
Set down by th' poll?
    Æd.   I have; 'tis ready here.
    Sic. Have you collected them by tribes?
    Æd.   I have.
    Sic. Assemble presently the people hither:
And, when they hear me say, *It shall be so*
I' the right and strength o' the commons, be it either
For death, for fine, or banishment, then let them,
If I say fine, cry *Fine;* if death, cry *Death;*
Insisting on the old prerogative
And power i' the truth o' the cause.
    Æd.   I shall inform them.
    Bru. And, when such time they have begun to cry,

---

[1] *Envy* is *hatred* or *malice* here, as commonly in Shakespeare.

Let them not cease, but with a din confused
Enforce the present execution
Of what we chance to sentence.

    Æd.   Very well.

    Sic. Make them be strong, and ready for this hint,
When we shall hap to give't them.

    Bru.   Go about it. —[*Exit Ædile.*
Put him to choler straight : he hath been used
Ever to conquer, and to have his word
Of contradiction : being once chafed, he cannot
Be rein'd again to temperance ; then he speaks
What's in his heart ; and that is there which looks
With us to break his neck.[2]

    Sic.   Well, here he comes.

  Enter CORIOLANUS, MENENIUS, COMINIUS, Senators, *and*
                    Patricians.

    Men. Calmly, I do beseech you.

    Cor. Ay, as an ostler, that for th' poorest piece
Will bear the knave by th' volume.[3] — Th' honour'd gods
Keep Rome in safety, and the chairs of justice
Supplied with worthy men ! plant love among's !
Throng our large temples with the shows of peace,
And not our streets with war !

    1 Sen.   Amen, amen !

    Men. A noble wish !

       Re-enter ÆDILE, *with* Citizens.

    Sic. Draw near, ye people.

---

  [2] " That which, with the use that we shall make of it, *tends,* or *is likely,*
to break his neck "; that is, hurl him from the Tarpeian rock.

  [3] Bear being called a knave as many times as would fill a volume.

Æd. List to your tribunes ; audience ! peace, I say !

Cor. First hear me speak.

Both Tri.   Well, say. — Peace, ho !

Cor. Shall I be charged no further than this present?
Must all determine here?

Sic.   I do demand,
If you submit you to the people's voices,
Allow their officers, and are content
To suffer lawful censure for such faults
As shall be proved upon you?

Cor.   I'm content.

Men. Lo, citizens, he says he is content :
The warlike service he has done, consider ; think
Upon the wounds his body bears, which show
Like graves i' the holy churchyard.

Cor.   Scratches with briers,
Scars to move laughter only.

Men.   Consider further,
That when he speaks not like a citizen,
You find him like a soldier : do not take
His rougher accents for malicious sounds,
But, as I say, such as become a soldier,
Rather than envy you.[4]

Com.   Well, well, no more.

Cor. What is the matter,
That, being pass'd for Consul with full voice,
I'm so dishonour'd, that the very hour
You take it off again?

Sic.   Answer to us.

Cor. Say, then ; 'tis true, I ought so.

---

[4] " Rather than such as spring from a purpose to *malign* or *spite* you."

Sic. We charge you, that you have contrived to take
From Rome all season'd office, and to wind
Yourself into a power tyrannical;
For which you are a traitor to the people.

Cor. How! traitor!

Men. Nay, temperately; your promise.

Cor. The fires i' the lowest Hell fold-in the people!
Call me their traitor? Thou injurious tribune!
Within thine eyes sat twenty thousand deaths,
In thy hands clutch'd as many millions, in
Thy lying tongue both numbers, I would say
Thou liest unto thee with a voice as free
As I do pray the gods.

Sic. Mark you this, people?

Citizens. To th' rock, to th' rock with him!

Sic. Peace!
We need not put new matter to his charge:
What you have seen him do and heard him speak,
Beating your officers, cursing yourselves,
Opposing laws with strokes, and here defying
Those whose great power must try him; even this
So criminal, and in such capital kind,
Deserves th' extremest death.

Bru. But, since he hath
Served well for Rome, —

Cor. What do you prate of service?

Bru. I talk of that that know it.

Cor. You!

Men. Is this the promise that you made your mother?

Com. Know, I pray you, —

Cor. I'll know no further:
Let them pronounce the steep Tarpeian death,

Vagabond exile, flaying, pent to linger
But with a grain a day, I would not buy
Their mercy at the price of one fair word;
Nor check my courage [5] for what they can give,
To have't with saying *Good morrow.*

   Sic.   For that he has,
As much as in him lies, from time to time
Inveigh'd against the people, seeking means
To pluck away their power; as [6] now at last
Given hostile strokes, and that not [7] in the presence
Of dreadful justice, but on the ministers
That do distribute it; in the name o' the people,
And in the power of us the tribunes, we,
Even from this instant, banish him our city;
In peril of precipitation
From off the rock Tarpeian, never more
To enter our Rome gates: i' the people's name,
I say it shall be so.

   Citizens.   It shall be so,
It shall be so; let him away: he's banish'd,
And it shall be so.

   Com. Hear me, my masters and my common friends, —
   Sic. He's sentenced; no more hearing.
   Com.   Let me speak:
I have been Consul, and can show for Rome
Her enemies' marks upon me.   I do love

---

  [5] *Courage* must here be taken in the sense of *spirit* or *resolution;* there being no apparent reason why Coriolanus should here speak of his *bravery,* as the people have not made this any ground of complaint.

  [6] *As* may here signify *as well as:* such elliptical modes of expression are not uncommon in Shakespeare.

  [7] *Not* is here again used for *not only.* See page 125, note 11.

My country's good with a respect more tender,
More holy, and profound, than mine own life,
My dear wife's estimate, her womb's increase,
And treasure of my loins ; then if I would
Speak that, —

    Sic.   We know your drift : speak what ?

    Bru. There's no more to be said, but he is banish'd,
As enemy to the people and his country :
It shall be so.

    Citizens.   It shall be so, it shall be so.

    Cor. You common cry of curs ![8] whose breath I hate
As reek o' the rotten fens, whose loves I prize
As the dead carcasses of unburied men
That do corrupt my air, I banish you :
And here remain with your uncertainty !
Let every feeble rumour shake your hearts !
Your enemies, wi' th' nodding of their plumes,
Fan you into despair !   Have the power still
To banish your defenders ; till at length
Your ignorance, which finds not till it feels,
Making but reservation of yourselves,[9]
Still your own foes, deliver you, as most
Abated[10] captives, to some nation

---

    [8] *Cry* here signifies a *pack.* So in a subsequent scene : " You have made
good work, you and your *cry.*" A *cry* of hounds was the old term for a
pack. See *Hamlet*, page 145, note 43.

    [9] Coriolanus imprecates upon the plebeians that they may still retain the
power of banishing their *defenders*, till their undiscerning folly, which can
foresee no consequences, leave none in the city *but themselves ;* so that, for
want of those capable of conducting their defence, they may fall an easy
prey to some nation who may conquer them without a struggle.

    [10] *Abated* is *overthrown, depressed.* To *abate* castles and houses, is to
overthrow them. To *abate* the courage of a man was to *depress* it.

That won you without blows! Despising, then,
For you, the city, thus I turn my back:
There is a world elsewhere.[11]

                    [*Exeunt* CORIOLANUS, COMINIUS, MENENIUS,
                              Senators, *and* Patricians.

  Æd. The people's enemy is gone, is gone!

  Citizens. Our enemy is banish'd! he is gone!

Hoo! hoo!   [*Shouting, and throwing up their caps.*

  Sic. Go, see him out at gates, and follow him,
As he hath follow'd you, with all despite;
Give him deserved vexation. Let a guard
Attend us through the city.

  Citizens. Come, come, let's see him out at gates; come,
    come;—

The gods preserve our noble tribunes!—come.   [*Exeunt.*

ACT IV.

SCENE I. — *Rome. Before a Gate of the City.*

Enter CORIOLANUS, VOLUMNIA, VIRGILIA, MENENIUS, COMINIUS
          and several young Patricians.

  Cor. Come, leave your tears; a brief farewell: the beast
With many heads butts me away. Nay, mother,
Where is your ancient courage? you were used

---

[11] It is remarkable that, among the political maxims of the speculative
Harrington, there is one that he might have borrowed from this speech:
"*The people cannot see, but they can feel.*" It is not much to the honour of
the people, that they have the same character of stupidity from their enemy
and their friend. Such was the power of our author's mind, that he looked
through life in all its relations private and civil. — JOHNSON.

To say extremity was the trier of spirits;
That common chances common men could bear;   .
That, when the sea was calm, all boats alike
Show'd mastership in floating; fortune's blows,
When most struck home, being gentle-minded craves
A noble cunning: [1] you were used to load me
With precepts that would make invincible
The heart that conn'd them.

  Vir. O Heavens! O Heavens!

  Cor.   Nay, I pr'ythee, woman, —

  Vol. Now the red pestilence strike all trades in Rome,
And occupations [2] perish!

  Cor.   What, what, what!
I shall be loved when I am lack'd.   Nay, mother,
Resume that spirit, when you were wont to say,
If you had been the wife of Hercules,
Six of his labours you'd have done, and saved
Your husband so much sweat. — Cominius,
Droop not; adieu. — Farewell, my wife, — my mother:
I'll do well yet. — Thou old and true Menenius,
Thy tears are salter than a younger man's,
And venomous to thine eyes. — My sometime general,
I've seen thee stern, and thou hast oft beheld
Heart-hardening spectacles: tell these sad women,
'Tis fond [3] to wail inevitable strokes,

---

[1] "When fortune's blows are most struck home, to bear them with a sweet and quiet mind requires a noble *wisdom*."   *Cunning* was often used for *wisdom* or *skill*.   "*Being* gentle-minded" has the force of "*to be* gentle-minded"; the participle for the infinitive.

[2] *Occupation* is used repeatedly by Shakespeare for *trade*, the trade of mechanics and artisans.   So in a subsequent scene: "You that stood so much upon the voice of *occupation*, and the breath of garlic-eaters."

[3] Here, as usual in Shakespeare, *fond* is *foolish*.

As 'tis to laugh at 'em. — My mother, you wot well
My hazards still have been your solace : and
Believe't not lightly, — though I go alone,
Like to a lonely dragon, that his fen [4]
Makes fear'd and talk'd of more than seen, — your son
Will or exceed the common, or be caught
With cautelous [5] baits and practice.

Vol.   My fair son,
Whither wilt thou go?   Take good Cominius
With thee awhile : determine on some course,
More than a wild exposure to each chance
That starts i' the way before thee.

Cor.   O the gods !

Com.   I'll follow thee a month, devise with thee
Where thou shalt rest, that thou mayst hear of us,
And we of thee : so, if the time thrust forth
A cause for thy repeal, we shall not send
O'er the vast world to seek a single man ;
And lose advantage, which doth ever cool
I' the absence of the needer.

Cor.   Fare ye well :
Thou'st years upon thee ; and thou art too full
Of the wars' surfeits, to go rove with one
That's yet unbruised : bring me but out at gate. —
Come, my sweet wife, my dearest mother, and
My friends of noble touch ; [6] when I am forth,

[4] The *fen* is the dragon's pestilential abode, which is talked of and shunned.

[5] *Cautelous* is *crafty, subtle, insidious.*   Warburton says that *cautel* " signified only a prudent foresight or caution, but, passing through French hands, it lost its innocence, and now signifies fraud, deceit." — *Common*, in the preceding line, has *hazards* understood.

[6] Of *true metal*.   The metaphor from the touchstone for trying metals is common in Shakespeare.

Bid me farewell, and smile.   I pray you, come.
While I remain above the ground, you shall
Hear from me still : and never of me aught
But what is like me formerly.

Men. That's worthily
As any ear can hear. —Come, let's not weep. —
If I could shake off but one seven years
From these old arms and legs, by the good gods,
I'd with thee every foot.

Cor. Give me thy hand :
Come. [*Exeunt.*

SCENE II. — *The Same.   A Street near the Gate.*

Enter SICINIUS, BRUTUS, *and an* Ædile.

Sic. Bid them all home ; he's gone, and we'll no
further.
The nobility are vex'd, who we see have sided
In his behalf.

Bru. Now we have shown our power,
Let us seem humbler after it is done
Than when it was a-doing.

Sic. Bid them home :
Say their great enemy is gone, and they
Stand in their ancient strength.

Bru. Dismiss them home. [*Exit* Ædile.
Here comes his mother.

Sic. Let's not meet her.

Bru. Why?

Sic. They say she's mad.

Bru. They have ta'en note of us : keep on your way.

Enter VOLUMNIA, VIRGILIA, *and* MENENIUS.

Vol. O, ye're well met : the hoarded plagues o' the gods
Requite your love ! [1]

Men.   Peace, peace ! be not so loud.

Vol. If that I could for weeping, you should hear, —
Nay, and you shall hear some. — [*To* BRUTUS.] Will you be
    gone ?

Vir. [*To* SICINIUS.] You shall stay too : I would I had
    the power
To say so to my husband.

Sic.   Are you mankind ? [2]

Vol. Ay, fool ; is that a shame ?   Note but this, fool :
Was not a man my father ?   Hadst thou foxship
To banish him that struck more blows for Rome
That thou hast spoken words ? —

Sic.   O blessèd Heavens !

Vol. More noble blows than ever thou wise words ;
And for Rome's good.   I'll tell thee what ; — yet go ; —
Nay, but thou shalt stay too : I would my son
Were in Arabia, and thy tribe before him,
His good sword in his hand.

Sic.   What then ?

Vol.   What then !
He'd make an end of thy posterity,
Bastards and all.   Good man, the wounds that he
Does bear for Rome !

Men. Come, come, peace !

---

[1] We have a like imprecation in *King Lear*, ii. 4 : " All the *stored ven-geances* of Heaven fall on her ingrateful top ! "

[2] " Are you a *man ?* " implying, of course, that she is somewhat viraginous. She kills the insult by ignoring it, choosing to understand him as asking whether she be human.   See *The Winter's Tale*, page 78, note 8.

Sic. I would he had continued to his country
As he began, and not unknit himself
The noble knot he made.

  Bru.   I would he had.

  Vol. I would he had ! 'Twas you incensed the rabble ;
Cats,[3] that can judge as fitly of his worth
As I can of those mysteries which Heaven
Will not have Earth to know.

  Bru.   Pray, let us go.

  Vol. Now, pray, sir, get you gone :
You've done a brave deed.   Ere you go, hear this :
As far as doth the Capitol exceed
The meanest house in Rome, so far my son, —
This lady's husband here, this, do you see, —
Whom you have banish'd, does exceed you all.

  Bru. Well, well, we'll leave you.

  Sic.   Why stay we to be baited
With one that wants her wits ?[4]

  Vol.   Take my prayers with you. —

            [Exeunt Tribunes.

I would the gods had nothing else to do
But to confirm my curses !   Could I meet 'em[5]
But once a-day, it would unclog my heart
Of what lies heavy to't.

  Men.   You've told them home ;
And, by my troth, you've cause.   You'll sup with me ?

  Vol. Anger's my meat ; I sup upon myself,
And so shall starve with feeding. — Come, let's go :

---

 [3] *Cats* is probably used of the Tribunes, not of the rabble, "*Ye* cats."

 [4] *Baited* is *barked at* or *worried*, as a bear by dogs.   See *Macbeth*, page
164, note 7. — " Baited *with* one " is old language for " baited *by* one."

 [5] " Could I meet the *tribunes*, and curse them " ; not meet the *gods*.

Leave this faint puling, and lament as I do,
In anger, Juno-like.   Come, come, come.

   Men.   Fie, fie, fie !

                                     [Exeunt.

SCENE III. — *A Highway between Rome and Antium.*

Enter a Roman *and a* Volsce, *meeting.*

   Rom. I know you well, sir, and you know me : your name,
I think, is Adrian.

   Vols. It is so, sir : truly, I have forgot you.

   Rom. I am a Roman ; and my services are, as you are,
against 'em : know you me yet?

   Vols. Nicanor? no.

   Rom. The same, sir.

   Vols. You had more beard when I last saw you ; but your
favour is well appear'd by your tongue.[1]   What's the news
in Rome?   I have a note from the Volscian State, to find you
out there : you have well saved me a day's journey.

   Rom. There hath been in Rome strange insurrections ;
the people against the Senators, patricians, and nobles.

   Vols. Hath been ! is it ended, then?   Our State thinks
not so : they are in a most warlike preparation, and hope to
come upon them in the heat of their division.

   Rom. The main blaze of it is past, but a small thing
would make it flame again ; for the nobles receive so to
heart the banishment of that worthy Coriolanus, that they
are in a ripe aptness to take all power from the people, and

---

[1] That is, "your *person* is well *shown* or *made apparent* by your *voice*."
The verb to *appear* is used repeatedly by the Poet in this way. See *Cymbe-*
line, page 138, note 8.

to pluck from them their tribunes for ever. This lies glow-
ing, I can tell you, and is almost mature for the violent
breaking out.

Vols. Coriolanus banish'd !

Rom. Banish'd, sir.

Vols. You will be welcome with this intelligence, Nicanor.

Rom. The day serves well for them now. I have heard
it said, the fittest time to corrupt a man's wife is when she's
fallen out with her husband. Your noble Tullus Aufidius
will appear well in these wars, his great opposer, Coriolanus,
being now in no request of his country.

Vols. He cannot choose. I am most fortunate, thus accidentally to encounter you : you have ended my business, and
I will merrily accompany you home.

Rom. I shall, between this and supper, tell you most
strange things from Rome ; all tending to the good of their
adversaries.   Have you an army ready, say you?

Vols. A most royal one ; the centurions and their charges,
distinctly billeted, already in the entertainment,[2] and to be on
foot at an hour's warning.

Rom. I am joyful to hear of their readiness, and am the
man, I think, that shall set them in present action. So, sir,
heartily well met, and most glad of your company.

Vols. You take my part from me, sir ; I have the most
cause to be glad of yours.

Rom. Well, let us go together.   [*Exeunt.*

---

2 " In the entertainment " is taken into the service, and on pay. — " *Dis-*
tinctly billeted " is assigned quarters, or lodgings, *separately ;* each company
by itself.   See *Othello*, page 109, note 34.

SCENE IV. — *Antium.　Before* AUFIDIUS'S *House.*

Enter CORIOLANUS *in mean apparel, disguised and muffled.*

Cor. A goodly city is this Antium. — City,
'Tis I that made thy widows : many an heir
Of these fair edifices 'fore my wars
Have I heard groan and drop : then know me not ;
Lest that thy wives with spits, and boys with stones,
In puny battle slay me. —

Enter a Citizen.

Save you, sir.
Cit. And you.
Cor.　　　　　Direct me, if it be your will,
Where great Aufidius lies : is he in Antium ?
Cit. He is, and feasts the nobles of the State
At his house this night.
Cor.　　　　　Which is his house, beseech you ?
Cit. This, here, before you.
Cor.　　　　　Thank you, sir : farewell. —
　　　　　　　　　　[*Exit* Citizen.
O world, thy slippery turns ! Friends now fast sworn,
Whose double bosoms seem to wear one heart,
Whose house, whose bed, whose meal, and exercise,
Are still together, who twin, as 'twere, in love
Unseparable, shall within this hour,
On a dissension of a doit, break out
To bitterest enmity : so, fellest foes,
Whose passions and whose plots have broke their sleep
To take the one the other, by some chance,

Some trick not worth an egg, shall grow dear friends,
And interjoin their issues.   So with me :
My birth-place hate I, and my love's upon
This enemy's town.   I'll enter : if he slay me,
He does fair justice ; if he give me way,
I'll do his country service.   [*Exit.*

SCENE V. — *The Same.   A Hall in* AUFIDIUS'S *House.*

Music within.   Enter a Servant.

1 Serv. Wine, wine, wine ! — What service is here ! I
think our fellows are asleep.   [*Exit.*

Enter a second Servant.

2 Serv. Where's Cotus? my master calls for him. —
Cotus !   [*Exit.*

Enter CORIOLANUS.

Cor. A goodly house : the feast smells well ; but I
Appear not like a guest.

Re-enter the first Servant.

1 Serv. What would you have, friend? whence are you?
Here's no place for you : pray, go to the door.   [*Exit.*
Cor. I have deserved no better entertainment
In being Coriolanus.[1]

Re-enter the second Servant.

2 Serv. Whence are you, sir? — Has the porter no eyes
in his head, that he gives entrance to such companions? —
Pray, get you out.

---

[1] In having gained that surname by the capture of Corioli.

Cor. Away !

2 Serv. Away ! get you away.

Cor. Now thou'rt troublesome.

2 Serv. Are you so brave? I'll have you talk'd with anon.

Enter a third Servant.

3 Serv. What fellow's this?

2 Serv. A strange one as ever I look'd on : I cannot get him out o' the house : pr'ythee, call my master to him.

3 Serv. What have you to do here, fellow? Pray you avoid the house.

Cor. Let me but stand ; I will not hurt your hearth.

3 Serv. What are you?

Cor. A gentleman.

3 Serv. A marvellous poor one.

Cor. True, so I am.

3 Serv. Pray you, poor gentleman, take up some other station ; here's no place for you ; pray you, avoid : come.

Cor. Follow your function, go, and batten [2] on cold bits.

[*Pushes him away.*

3 Serv. What, you will not? — Pr'ythee, tell my master what a strange guest he has here.

2 Serv. And I shall.   [*Exit.*

3 Serv. Where dwellest thou?

Cor. Under the canopy.

3 Serv. Under the canopy !

Cor. Ay.

3 Serv. Where's that?

Cor. I' the city of kites and crows.

---

[2] To *batten* is to *feed coarsely* or *grossly*. So in *Hamlet*, iii. 4 : "Could you on this fair mountain leave to feed, and *batten* on this moor?"

3 Serv. I' the city of kites and crows!—What an ass it is!—Then thou dwell'st with daws too?

Cor. No, I serve not thy master.

Serv. How, sir! do you meddle with my master?

Cor. Ay; 'tis honester service than to meddle with thy mistress:

Thou pratest, and pratest; serve with thy trencher, hence!

                                       [Beats him in.

Enter AUFIDIUS *with the second* Servant.

Auf. Where is this fellow?

2 Serv. Here, sir: I'd have beaten him like a dog, but for disturbing the lords within.   *[The two* Servants *retire.*

Auf. Whence comest thou? what wouldest thou? thy name?

Why speak'st not? speak, man: what's thy name?

Cor. [*Unmuffling.*]   If, Tullus,

Not yet thou knowest me, and, seeing me, dost not

Think me the man I am, necessity

Commands me name myself.

Auf.   What is thy name?

Cor. A name unmusical to th' Volscians' ears,

And harsh in sound to thine.

Auf.   Say, what's thy name?

Thou hast a grim appearance, and thy face

Bears a command in't; though thy tackle's torn,

Thou show'st a noble vessel: what's thy name?

Cor. Prepare thy brow to frown. Know'st thou me yet?

Auf. I know thee not: thy name?

Cor. My name is Caius Marcius, who hath done

To thee particularly and to all the Volsces

Great hurt and mischief; thereto witness may

My surname, Coriolanus : the painful service,
The éxtreme dangers, and the drops of blood
Shed for my thankless country, are requited
But with that surname ; a good memory,[3]
And witness of the malice and displeasure
Which thou shouldst bear me.   Only that name remains :
The cruelty and envy of the people,
Permitted by our dastard nobles, who
Have all forsook me, hath devour'd the rest ;
And suffer'd me by th' voice of slaves to be
Whoop'd out of Rome.   Now, this extremity
Hath brought me to thy hearth ; not out of hope —
Mistake me not — to save my life ; for, if
I had fear'd death, of all the men i' the world
I would have 'voided thee ; but in mere spite,
To be full quit[4] of those my banishers,
Stand I before thee here.   Then, if thou hast
A heart of wreak[5] in thee, that will revenge
Thine own particular wrongs, and stop those maims
Of shame[6] seen through thy country, speed thee straight,
And make my misery serve thy turn : so use it,
That my revengeful services may prove
As benefits to thee ; for I will fight
Against my canker'd[7] country with the spleen

[3] *Memory* is here used for *memorial* or *reminder ;* that which recalls to memory.   A frequent usage.   See *King Lear*, page 186, note 2.

[4] *Quit* for *quited*, and in the sense of *requited ;* that is *avenged*.

[5] *Wreak* is an old term for *revenge*.   So in *Titus Andronicus :* " Take *wreak* on Rome for this ingratitude."

[6] " Maims of shame " is shameful maims ; probably meaning disreputable losses of territory.

[7] Shakespeare uses *canker*, noun and verb, in four distinct senses.   I am not quite clear in what sense it is used here ; probably in that of a malignant sore, like *cancer*.   See *Romeo and Juliet*, page 39, note 11.

Of all the under fiends.   But, if so be
Thou darest not this, and that to prove more fortunes
Thou'rt tired, then, in a word, I also am
Longer to live most weary, and present
My throat to thee and to thy ancient malice ;
Which not to cut would show thee but a fool,
Since I have ever follow'd thee with hate,
Drawn tuns of blood out of thy country's breast,
And cannot live but to thy shame, unless
It be to do thee service.

    Auf.   O Marcius, Marcius !
Each word thou hast spoke hath weeded from my heart
A root of ancient envy.   If Jupiter
Should from out yonder cloud speak divine things,
And say *'Tis true*, I'd not believe him more
Than thee, all-noble Marcius.   Let me twine
Mine arms about that body, where-against
My grainèd ash an hundred times hath broke,
And scarr'd the Moon with splinters : [8] here I clip
The anvil of my sword ; [9] and do contest
As hotly and as nobly with thy love
As ever in ambitious strength I did
Contend against thy valour.   Know, thou first,[10]
I loved the maid I married ; never man

---

[8] The idea, or the expression, of *scarring* the Moon is hyperbolical enough. We have a like expression in *King Richard III.*, v. 3 : "*Amaze the welkin* with your *broken staves.*"   See Critical Notes.

[9] To *clip* is to *embrace*. Repeatedly so. Aufidius calls Coriolanus the *anvil of his sword*, because he has in days past laid as heavy blows upon him as a smith strikes on his anvil.

[10] That is, thou first or *foremost of men*. As Mr. P. A. Daniel observes, "Aufidius addresses Coriolanus throughout in superlatives, — 'All-noble Marcius !' 'Thou noble thing !' 'Thou Mars !' 'Most absolute sir.' "

Sigh'd truer breath : but, that I see thee here,
Thou noble thing ! more dances my rapt heart
Than when I first my wedded mistress saw
Bestride my threshold. Why, thou Mars ! I tell thee,
We have a power on foot ; and I had purpose
Once more to hew thy target from thy brawn,
Or lose mine arm for't : thou hast beat me out [11]
Twelve several times, and I have nightly since
Dreamt of encounters 'twixt thyself and me ;
We have been down together in my sleep,
Unbuckling helms, fisting each other's throat,
And waked half dead with nothing.   Worthy Marcius
Had we no quarrel else to Rome, but that
Thou art thence banish'd, we would muster all
From twelve to seventy ; and, pouring war
Into the bowels of ungrateful Rome,
Like a bold flood o'er-bear.   O, come, go in,
And take our friendly Senators by th' hands ;
Who now are here taking their leaves of me,
Who am prepared against your territories,
Though not for Rome itself.
   Cor.   You bless me, gods !
   Auf. Therefore, most absolute sir, if thou wilt have
The leading of thine own revenges, take
Th' one half of my commission ; and set down —
As best thou art experienced, since thou know'st
Thy country's strength and weakness — thine own ways ;
Whether to knock against the gates of Rome,
Or rudely visit them in parts remote,
To fright them, ere destroy.   But come thou in :

---

[11] *Out* for *outright*, as we should say ; that is, *thoroughly*.

Let me commend thee first to those that shall
Say yea to thy desires.   A thousand welcomes !
And more a friend than e'er an enemy ;
Yet, Marcius, that was much.   Your hand : most welcome !

> [*Exeunt* CORIOLANUS *and* AUFIDIUS. — *The*
> *two* Servants *come forward.*

1 Serv. Here's a strange alteration !

2 Serv. By my hand, I had thought to have strucken him
with a cudgel ; and yet my mind gave me his clothes made
a false report of him.

1 Serv. What an arm he has ! he turn'd me about with his
finger and his thumb as one would set up a top.

2 Serv. Nay, I knew by his face that there was something
in him : he had, sir, a kind of face, methought, — I cannot
tell how to term it.

1 Serv. He had so ; looking as it were, — Would I were
hang'd, but I thought there was more in him than I could think.

2 Serv. So did I, I'll be sworn : he is simply the rarest
man i' the world.

1 Serv. I think he is ; but a greater soldier than he you
wot on.

2 Serv. Who? my master ?

1 Serv. Nay, it's no matter for that.

2 Serv. Worth six on him.

1 Serv. Nay, not so neither ; but I take him to be the
greater soldier.

2 Serv. Faith, look you, one cannot tell how to say that :
for the defence of a town our general is excellent.

1 Serv. Ay, and for an assault too.

Re-enter the third Servant.

3 Serv. O slaves, I can tell you news, —news, you rascals !

1 and 2 Serv. What, what, what? let's partake.

3 Serv. I would not be a Roman, of all nations; I had as lief be a condemn'd man.

1 and 2 Serv. Wherefore? wherefore?

3 Serv. Why, here's he that was wont to thwack our general, — Caius Marcius.

1 Serv. Why do you say *thwack our general?*

3 Serv. I do not say *thwack our general;* but he was always good enough for him.

2 Serv. Come, we are fellows and friends: he was ever too hard for him; I have heard him say so himself.

1 Serv. He was too hard for him directly, to say the troth on't: before Corioli he scotch'd him and notch'd him like a carbonado.

2 Serv. An he had been cannibally given, he might have broil'd and eaten him too.

1 Serv. But, more of thy news.

3 Serv. Why, he is so made on here within as if he were son and heir to Mars; set at upper end o' the table; no question ask'd him by any of the Senators, but they stand bald before him: our general himself makes a mistress of him; sanctifies himself with's hand,[12] and turns up the white o' the eye to his discourse. But the bottom of the news is, our general is cut i' the middle, and but one half of what he was yesterday; for the other has half, by the entreaty and grant of the whole table. He'll go, he says, and sowl[13] the

[12] Considers the touch of his hand as holy; clasps it with the same reverence as a lover would clasp the hand of his mistress.

[13] To *sowl* is to pull by the ears. It is still provincially in use for pulling, dragging, or lugging. Heywood uses it in his comedy called *Love's Mistress*, 1636: "Venus will *sowle* me by the ears for this." And in a letter from Mr. Garrard to Lord Strafford: "A lieutenant *soled him well by the ears*, and drew him by the hair about the room."

porter of Rome gates by th' ears: he will mow all down before him, and leave his passage poll'd.[14]

2 Serv. And he's as like to do't as any man I can imagine.

3 Serv. Do't! he will do't; for, look you, sir, he has as many friends as enemies; which friends, sir, as it were, durst not, look you, sir, show themselves, as we term it, his friends whilst he's in directitude.[15]

1 Serv. Directitude! what's that?

3 Serv. But, when they shall see, sir, his crest up again, and the man in blood, they will out of their burrows, like conies after rain, and revel all with him.

1 Serv. But when goes this forward?

3 Serv. To-morrow; to-day; presently; you shall have the drum struck up this afternoon: 'tis, as it were, a parcel of their feast, and to be executed ere they wipe their lips.

2 Serv. Why, then we shall have a stirring world again. This peace is nothing, but to rust iron, increase tailors, and breed ballad-makers.

1 Serv. Let me have war, say I; it exceeds peace as far as day does night; it's sprightly, waking, audible, and full of vent.[16] Peace is a very apoplexy, a lethargy; mute, deaf, sleepy, insensible: and it makes men hate one another.

---

[14] To *poll* is to *crop close*, to *shear*; and has all the figurative meanings of *tondo* in Latin. To *pill* and *poll* was to *plunder* and *strip*.

[15] Probably meant as a blunder for *discreditude*; the servant endeavouring to say something very grand and fine.

[16] *Full of vent* has puzzled the editors vastly; and we are at last indebted to *The Edinburgh Review*, October, 1872, for what seems a right explanation of it: "*Vent* is a technical term in hunting, to express the scenting of the game by the hounds employed in the chase." This the writer shows by the following quotations from a popular manual of hunting in Shakespeare's day: "My liege, I went this morning on my quest; My hound did sticke,

3 Serv. Reason; because they then less need one another. The wars for my money. I hope to see Romans as
cheap as Volscians. They are rising, they are rising.

All Three. In, in, in, in! 　　　　　　　　　[*Exeunt.*

SCENE VI. — *Rome.　A public Place.*

Enter SICINIUS *and* BRUTUS.

Sic. We hear not of him, neither need we fear him;
His remedies are tame: the present peace
And quietness of the people, which before
Were in wild hurry, here do make his friends
Blush that the world goes well; who rather had,
Though they themselves did suffer by't, behold
Dissentious numbers pestering streets, than see
Our tradesmen singing in their shops, and going
About their functions friendly.

Bru. We stood to't in good time. Is this Menenius?

Sic. 'Tis he, 'tis he: O, he is grown most kind
Of late. —

Enter MENENIUS.

　　　　　　Hail, sir!

Bru. 　　　　　　　　　Hail, sir!

Men. 　　　　　　　　　　　　Hail to you both!

Sic. Your Coriolanus, sir, is not much miss'd
But with his friends: the commonwealth doth stand;

and seemed to *vent* some beast." And again: "And when my hound doth
straine upon good *vent*, I must confesse the same doth me content." The
writer then adds: "To strain at the leash 'upon good *vent*' is, in Shakespeare's phrase, to be 'full of vent'"; or, in other words, keenly excited, full
of pluck and courage, of throbbing energy and impetuous desire; in a word,
full of all the kindling stir and commotion of anticipated conflict.

And so would do, were he more angry at it.

Men. All's well ; and might have been much better, if
He could have temporized.[1]

Sic.   Where is he, hear you?

Men. Nay, I hear nothing : his mother and his wife
Hear nothing from him.

Enter three or four Citizens.

Citizens. The gods preserve you both !

Sic.   God-den,[2] our neighbours.

Bru. God-den to you all, god-den to you all.

1 Cit. Ourselves, our wives, and children, on our knees,
Are bound to pray for both you.

Sic.   Live, and thrive !

Bru. Farewell, kind neighbours : we wish'd Coriolanus
Had loved you as we did.

Citizens.   Now the gods keep you !

Both Trib. Farewell, farewell.   [*Exeunt* Citizens.

Sic. This is a happier and more comely time
Than when these fellows ran about the streets
Crying confusion.

Bru.   Caius Marcius was
A worthy officer i' the war ; but insolent,
O'ercome with pride, ambitious past all thinking,
Self-loving, —

Sic.   And affecting [3] one sole throne,

---

1 To *temporize* is to comply with the exigencies of the time ; or to dis-
semble, to play Sir Prudence, and so abide one's time. See *The Winter's
Tale*, page 54, note 45.

2 *God-den* or *good den*, is an old colloquialism for *good even* or *good day*.
The Poet has it repeatedly. See *Romeo and Juliet*, page 86, note 23.

3 To *affect* a thing, as the word is here used, is to *crave* it, to *have a passion for* it. See *King Henry the Eighth*, page 45, note 10.

Without assistance.

Men.   Nay, I think not so.

Sic. We should by this, to all our lamentation,
If he had gone forth Consul, so have found it.

Bru. The gods have well prevented it, and Rome
Sits safe and still without him.

Enter an Ædile.

Æd.   Worthy tribunes,
There is a slave, whom we have put in prison,
Reports, the Volsces with two several powers
Are enter'd in the Roman territories,
And with the deepest malice of the war
Destroy what lies before 'em.

Men.   'Tis Aufidius,
Who, hearing of our Marcius' banishment,
Thrusts forth his horns again into the world ;
Which were inshell'd when Marcius stood for Rome,
And durst not once peep out.

Sic.   Come, what talk you
Of Marcius?

Bru. Go see this rumourer whipp'd. — It cannot be
The Volsces dare break with us.

Men.   Cannot be !
We have recórd that very well it can ;
And three examples of the like have been
Within my age.   But reason [4] with the fellow,
Before you punish him, where he heard this ;
Lest you shall chance to whip your information,
And beat the messenger who bids beware
Of what is to be dreaded.

---

[4] To *reason*, again, for to *talk* or *converse*. See page 69, note 9.

Sic.   Tell not me :
I know this cannot be.
   Bru.   Not possible.

Enter a Messenger.

Mess. The nobles in great earnestness are going
All to the Senate-house : some news is come
That turns their countenances.
   Sic.   'Tis this slave ; —
Go whip him 'fore the people's eyes ; — his raising ;
Nothing but his report.
   Mess.   Yes, worthy sir,
The slave's report is seconded ; and more,
More fearful, is deliver'd.
   Sic.   What more fearful?
   Mess. It is spoke freely out of many mouths —
How probable I do not know — that Marcius,
Join'd with Aufidius, leads a power 'gainst Rome,
And vows revenge as spacious as between
The young'st and oldest thing.[5]
   Sic.   This is most likely !
   Bru. Raised only, that the weaker sort may wish
Good Marcius home again.
   Sic.   The very trick on't.
   Men. This is unlikely :
He and Aufidius can no more atone[6]
Than violentest contrarieties.

Enter a second Messenger.

2 Mess. You are sent for to the Senate :

---

[5] So comprehensive as to include all, from the youngest to the oldest.
[6] To *atone* is to *unite* or *be reconciled*, to *at-one*.   Repeatedly so.

A fearful army, led by Caius Marcius
Associated with Aufidius, rages
Upon our territories ; and have already
O'erborne their way, consumed with fire, and took
What lay before them.

Enter COMINIUS:

  Com. O, you have made good work !
  Men.   What news ? what news ?
  Com. You've holp to ravish your own daughters, and
To melt the city leads upon your pates ;
To see your wives dishonour'd to your noses ; —
  Men. What's the news ? what's the news ?
  Com. — Your temples burnèd in their cement ;[7] and
Your franchises, whereon you stood, confined
Into[8] an auger's bore.
  Men.   Pray now, your news ? —
You've made fair work, I fear me. — Pray, your news ?
If Marcius should be join'd wi' th' Volscians, —
  Com.   If !
He is their god : he leads them like a thing
Made by some other deity than Nature,
That shapes man better ; and they follow him,
Against us brats, with no less confidence
Than boys pursuing summer butterflies,
Or butchers killing flies.
  Men.   You've made good work,
You and your apron-men ; you that stood so much

---

  [7] "*In* for *into :* the very walls penetrated and crumbled by the fire." So
says Mr. Whitelaw : Heath explains it, "Burned with whatever serves to
cement and hold them together."

  [8] *Into* for *within ;* as, just before, *in* for *into.* See *Tempest*, page 63, note 73.

Upon the voice of occupation and
The breath of garlic-eaters![9]

Com.   He will shake
Your Rome about your ears.

Men.   As Hercules
Did shake down mellow fruit.[10] — You've made fair work !

Bru. But is this true, sir ?

Com.   Ay ; and you'll look pale
Before you find it other.   All the regions
Do smilingly revolt ; and who resist
Are mock'd for valiant ignorance,
And perish constant fools.   Who is't can blame him ?
Your enemies and his find something in him.

Men. We are all undone, unless
The noble man have mercy.

Com.   Who shall ask it ?
The tribunes cannot do't for shame ; the people
Deserve such pity of him as the wolf
Does of the shepherds : for his best friends, if they
Should say, *Be good to Rome*, they charged him even
As those should do that had deserved his hate,
And therein show'd like enemies.[11]

Men.   'Tis true :
If he were putting to my house the brand
That should consume it, I have not the face
To say, *'Beseech you, cease.* — You've made fair hands,
You and your crafts ! you've crafted fair !

---

[9] To smell of *garlic* was a brand of vulgarity ; as to smell of leeks was no less so among the Roman people.

[10] A ludicrous allusion to the apples of Hesperides.

[11] " They *charged*, and therein *show'd*," has here the force of " they *would charge*, and therein *show*."

Com.   You've brought
A trembling upon Rome, such as was never
So incapable of help.

   Both Trib.   Say not, we brought it.

   Men. How ! Was it we? we loved him ; but, like beasts
And cowardly nobles, gave way unto your clusters,
Who did hoot him out o' the city.

   Com.   But I fear
They'll roar him in again.   Tullus Aufidius,
The second name of men, obeys his points [12]
As if he were his officer : desperation
Is all the policy, strength, and defence,
That Rome can make against them.

Enter a troop of Citizens.

   Men.   Here come the clusters.
And is Aufidius with him? — You are they
That made the air unwholesome, when you cast
Your stinking greasy caps in hooting at
Coriolanus' exile.   Now he's coming ;
And not a hair upon a soldier's head
Which will not prove a whip : as many coxcombs
As you threw caps up will he tumble down,
And pay you for your voices.   'Tis no matter ;
If he could burn us all into one coal,
We have deserved it.

   Citizens. Faith, we hear fearful news.

   1 Cit.   For mine own part,
When I said, banish him, I said, 'twas pity.

   2 Cit. And so did I.

---

[12] *Points* probably means the same here as in *The Tempest*, i. 2 : " But
then exactly do all *points* of my command."

3 Cit. And so did I ; and, to say the truth, so did very many of us : that we did, we did for the best ; and though we willingly consented to his banishment, yet it was against our will.

Com. Ye're goodly things, you voices !

Men.   You have made Good work, you and your cry ! [13] — Shall's to the Capitol ?

Com. O, ay, what else ?   [*Exeunt* COMIN. *and* MENEN.

Sic. Go, masters, get you home ; be not dismay'd : These are a side that would be glad to have This true which they so seem to fear.   Go home, And show no sign of fear.

1 Cit. The gods be good to us ! — Come, masters, let's home.   I ever said we were i' the wrong when we banish'd him.

2 Cit. So did we all.   But, come, let's home.

                                        [*Exeunt* Citizens.

Bru. I do not like this news.

Sic. Nor I.

Bru. Let's to the Capitol.   Would half my wealth Would buy this for a lie !

Sic.   Pray, let us go.   [*Exeunt.*

SCENE VII. — *A Camp, at a small distance from Rome.*

Enter AUFIDIUS *and his* Lieutenant.

Auf. Do they still fly to th' Roman ?

Lieu. I do not know what witchcraft's in him, but Your soldiers use him as the grace 'fore meat,

---

[13] *Cry* for *pack*, as before.   See page 134, note 8.

Their talk at table, and their thanks at end ;
And you are darken'd in this action, sir,
Even by your own.

    Auf.   I cannot help it now,
Unless, by using means, I lame the foot
Of our design. He bears himself more proudlier,
Even to my person, than I thought he would
When first I did embrace him : yet his nature
In that's no changeling ; and I must excuse
What cannot be amended.

    Lieu.   Yet I wish, sir, —
I mean for your particular, — you had not
Join'd in commission with him ; but either
Had borne the action of yourself, or else
To him had left it solely.

    Auf. I understand thee well ; and be thou sure,
When he shall come to his account, he knows not
What I can urge against him. Although it seems,
And so he thinks, and is no less apparent
To th' vulgar eye, that he bears all things fairly,
And shows good husbandry for th' Volscian State,
Fights dragon-like, and does achieve as soon
As draw his sword ; yet he hath left undone
That which shall break his neck or hazard mine,
Whene'er we come to our account.

    Lieu. Sir, I beseech you, think you he'll carry Rome ?

    Auf. All places yield to him ere he sits down ;
And the nobility of Rome are his ;
The Senators and patricians love him too ;
The tribunes are no soldiers ; and their people
Will be as rash in the repeal, as hasty
T' expel him thence. I think he'll be to Rome

As is the osprey to the fish,[1] who takes it
By sovereignty of nature.　First he was
A noble servant to them ; but he could not
Carry his honours even : whether 'twas pride,
Which out of daily fortune ever taints
The happy man ;[2] whether defect of judgment,
To fail in the disposing of those chances
Which he was lord of ; or whether nature, .
Not to be other than one thing, not moving
From th' casque to th' cushion,[3] but commanding peace
Even with the same austerity and garb
As he controll'd the war ; but one of these —
As he hath spices of them all, not all,[4]
For I dare so far free him — made him fear'd,
So hated, and so banish'd : but he has a merit,
To choke it in the utterance.[5]　So our virtues

---

[1] As fish, overcome by fear, or by a sort of fascination, surrender themselves to the osprey.　So in Peele's *Battle of Alcazar*, 1594 :

> I will provide thee with a princely osprey,
> That, as she flieth over fish in pools,
> The fish shall turn their glittering bellies up,
> And thou shalt take thy liberal choice of all.

[2] "The *happy* man" is the *fortunate* or the *prosperous* man.　Like the Latin *felix*.　Shakespeare has it repeatedly so.

[3] Aufidius assigns three probable reasons for the miscarriage of Coriolanus ; pride, which easily follows an uninterrupted train of success ; unskilfulness to regulate the consequences of his own victories ; a stubborn uniformity of nature, which could not make the proper transition from the *casque* to the *cushion* or *chair of civil authority ;* but acted with the same despotism in peace as in war. — JOHNSON.

[4] "He has a *touch* or *taste* of all the faults in question ; but has not them all *in their full force*, or not *altogether*."

[5] But his merit as a soldier is so great, that the very name of his fault must stick in the throat of his accusers.

Lie in th' interpretation of the time ;[6]
And power, unto itself most cómmendable,[7]
Hath not a tomb so evident as a chair,
T' extol what it hath done.[8]
One fire drives out one fire ;[9] one nail, one nail ;

[6] Our virtues depend, for their good name, on the particular exigencies in which we are called to act ; are virtues, or the reverse, according to the construction which the time puts upon them. So, in reference to the hero, that overbearing, domineering spirit, which is praised as a virtue in military command, will be resented as a vice in civil life. As Mr. Whitelaw well expresses it, " The soldier who is all soldier is misinterpreted in time of peace ; for his unfitness for peace is seen, his fitness for war is not seen."

[7] That is, the power which, having been nobly won in war, is therefore conscious of deserving well, and so commends itself unto itself, and can nowise understand why it should be odious or unfitting in time of peace. The idea running through the speech is, that the hero, carrying his military style and habits into civil life, and using his power so harshly as to provoke hatred, will become as intolerable to the Volscians after he has taken Rome as he did to the Romans after he had taken Corioli.

[8] Shakespeare repeatedly uses *evident* in the sense of *certain* or *inevitable*. So in the next scene : " We must find an *evident* calamity, though we had our wish, which side should win." *A chair* refers to the *sella curulis*, the distinctive official seat of the higher Roman magistracies. "A chair, *to extol*" is a chair *that extols ;* just as, a little before, " a merit, *to choke*" is a merit *that chokes*. The speaker's argument is, that Coriolanus, by his arrogance and tyranny in peace, will surely and speedily kill the popularity he has gained in war. And so the meaning here is, that power, joined to a haughty, domineering temper, and loved and gloried in for its own sake, *hath no grave so certain*, or so *imminent, as a chair of state bestowed in honour and extolment of its deeds*. Or, to put the matter in a concrete form, let Coriolanus, with his habits of military prerogative, and of lording it over all about him, be once advanced to a place of civil authority, and he will soon become an object of public hatred ; so that the very seat which rewards and blazons his exploits will be sure to prove his ruin and the tomb of his power. See Critical Notes.

[9] That is, heat expels heat ; alluding to the old notion of curing a burn by holding the burnt place up to the fire. Shakespeare has the same allusion repeatedly. So in *Julius Cæsar*, iii. 1 : " As *fire drives out fire*, so pity pity." See, also, *Romeo and Juliet*, page 47, note 5.

Rights by rights fouler, strengths by strengths, do fail.[10]
Come, let's away. — When, Caius, Rome is thine,
Thou'rt poor'st of all ; then shortly art thou mine. [*Exeunt.*

———————

ACT V.

Scene I. — *Rome.   A public Place.*

Enter Menenius, Cominius, Sicinius, Brutus, *and others.*

Men. No, I'll not go : you hear what he hath said
Which was sometime his general ; who loved him
In a most dear particular.   He call'd me father :
But what o' that? Go, you that banish'd him ;
A mile before his tent fall down, and knee
The way into his mercy : [1] nay, if he coy'd
To hear [2] Cominius speak, I'll keep at home.
    Com. He would not seem to know me.
    Men.   Do you hear?
    Com. Yet one time he did call me by my name :
I urged our old acquaintance, and the drops

———

[10] The meaning of this line, expressed in full, probably is, that the better
rights succumb to the worse, and the nobler strengths to the meaner ; the
sense of *fail* being anticipated in the first clause, and that of *fouler* continued over the second.   Here, as elsewhere, Aufidius is fully conscious
of the foulness of his purposes.   The only thing he cares for is to get a sure
twist on his antagonist.   See Critical Notes.

[1] To *knee* one's way is to go on one's *knees*, as to *foot* one's way is to go
on one's *feet*.   So, some one having remarked that Lord Malmesbury had
been a long time in getting to Paris, Burke is said to have replied, " No
wonder ; every step he took was on his knees."

[2] *Coy'd to hear* is the same as *was coy of hearing;* that is, was distant
and reserved, — was *shy and scrupulous of lending his ear.*

That we have bled together. *Coriolanus*
He would not answer to ; forbade all names ;
He was a kind of nothing, titleless,
Till he had forged himself a name o' the fire
Of burning Rome.

    Men.   Why, so ; you've made good work !
A pair of tribunes that have wreck'd fair Rome
To make coals cheap, — a noble memory ! [3]

    Com. I minded him how royal 'twas to pardon
When it was least expected : he replied,
It was a rare petition of a State
To one whom they had punish'd.

    Men.   Very well :
Could he say less ?

    Com. I offer'd to awaken his regard
For's private friends : his answer to me was,
He could not stay to pick them in a pile
Of noisome musty chaff : he said 'twas folly,
For one poor grain or two, to leave't unburnt,
And still to nose th' offence.

    Men.   For one poor grain or two !
I'm one of those ; his mother, wife, his child,
And this brave fellow too, we are the grains :
You are the musty chaff ; and you are smelt
Above the Moon : we must be burnt for you.

    Sic. Nay, pray, be patient : if you refuse your aid
In this so never-needed help, yet do not
Upbraid's with our distress.   But, sure, if you
Would be your country's pleader, your good tongue,

---

[3] The meaning is, "who have erected a noble *memorial* or *monument* for themselves by wrecking fair Rome in order to cheapen the price of fuel. We have had *memory* just so before.   See page 147, note 3.

More than the instant army we can make,[4]
Might stop our countryman.

    Men.   No, I'll not meddle.

    Sic. Pray you now, go to him.

    Men.   What should I do?

    Bru. Only make trial what your love can do
For Rome, towards Marcius.

    Men.   Well, and say that Marcius
Return me, as Cominius is return'd,
Unheard; what then? or not unheard, but as
A discontented friend, grief-shot with his
Unkindness?

    Sic.   Say't be so, yet your good will
Must have that thanks from Rome, after the measure
As you intended well.[5]

    Men.   I'll undertake't:
I think he'll hear me. Yet, to bite his lip
And hum at good Cominius, much unhearts me.
He was not taken well; he had not dined:
The veins unfill'd, our blood is cold, and then
We pout upon the morning, are unapt
To give or to forgive; but, when we've stuff'd
These pipes and these conveyances of our blood
With wine and feeding, we have suppler souls
Than in our priest-like fasts: therefore I'll watch him
Till he be dieted to my request,
And then I'll set upon him.

    Bru. You know the very road into his kindness,
And cannot lose your way.

---

[4] That is, the army we can levy on the instant, or *at present*.

[5] "Such gratitude as will accord with the measure of your good intentions." *After* often means *according to*.

Men.   Good faith, I'll prove him.
Speed how it will, you shall ere long have knowledge
Of my success.[6]   [*Exit.*

Com.   He'll never hear him.

Sic.   Not?

Com. I tell you, he does sit in gold,[7] his eye
Red as 'twould burn Rome ; and his injúry
The jailer to his pity.[8]   I kneel'd before him ;
'Twas very faintly he said *Rise ;* dismiss'd me
Thus, with his speechless hand : what he would do,
He sent in writing after me, what he would not ;
Bound with an oath to yield to his conditions : [9]
So that all hope is vain,
Unless in's noble mother and his wife ;
Who, as I hear, mean to solicit him
For mercy to his country.   Therefore let's hence,
And with our fair entreaties haste them on.   [*Exeunt.*

---

[6] *Success*, again, in its Latin sense of *result*.   See page 48, note 26.

[7] This is well explained from North's Plutarch : " He was set in his chair of state, with a marvellous and unspeakable majesty."

[8] His remembrance of the wrong done him kept his pity under lock and key.

[9] A passage hard to be understood at the best, and still more obscure as commonly pointed, thus : " What he would do, he sent in writing after me ; what he would not, bound with an oath, to yield to his conditions " : which is severing " what he would do " from " bound with an oath," and " what he would not " from " he sent in writing after me."   As here given the sense may be rendered thus : " He sent in writing after me both what he would do and what he would not ; binding the whole with an oath that we should yield to his conditions."   See Critical Notes.

SCENE II. — *An Outpost of the Volscian Camp before Rome.*
    The Sentinels *at their Stations.*

Enter to them MENENIUS.

1 Sen. Stay : whence are you?

2 Sen. Stand, and go back.

Men. You guard like men ; 'tis well : but, by your leave,
I am an officer of State, and come
To speak with Coriolanus.

1 Sen.   From whence?

Men.   From Rome.

1 Sen. You may not pass, you must return : our general
Will no more hear from thence.

2 Sen. You'll see your Rome embraced with fire, before
You'll speak with Coriolanus.

Men.   Good my friends,
If you have heard your general talk of Rome,
And of his friends there, it is lots to blanks [1]
My name hath touch'd your ears : it is Menenius.

1 Sen. Be't so ; go back : the virtue of your name
Is not here passable.

Men.   I tell thee, fellow,
Thy general is my lover : [2] I have been
The book of his good acts, whence men have read
His fame unparallel'd, haply amplified ;
For I have ever amplified my friends —
Of whom he's chief — with all the size that verity
Would without lapsing suffer : nay, sometimes,

---

[1] *Lots* to *blanks* is *chances* to *nothing.*

[2] The use of *lover* for *friend* was very common.

Like to a bowl upon a subtle [3] ground,
I've tumbled past the throw ; and in his praise
Have almost stamp'd the leasing : [4] therefore, fellow,
I must have leave to pass.

1 Sen. Faith, sir, if you had told as many lies in his behalf as you have uttered words in your own, you should not
pass here ; no, though were as virtuous to lie as to live
chastely. Therefore, go back.

Men. Pr'ythee, fellow, remember my name is Menenius,
always factionary [5] on the party of your general.

1 Sen. Howsoever you have been his liar, as you say you
have, I am one that, telling true under him, must say you
cannot pass. Therefore, go back.

Men. Has he dined, canst thou tell? for I would not speak
with him till after dinner.

1 Sen. You are a Roman, are you?

Men. I am, as thy general is.

1 Sen. Then you should hate Rome, as he does. Can
you, when you have push'd out your gates the very defender
of them, and, in a violent popular ignorance, given your
enemy your shield, think to front his revenges with the easy
groans of old women, the virginal palms [6] of your daughters,
or with the palsied intercession of such a decay'd dotant as
you seem to be? Can you think to blow out the intended
fire your city is ready to flame in with such weak breath as

---

[3] *Subtle* here means *smooth, level*. So in Ben Jonson's *Chlorida :*
"Tityus's breast is counted the *subtlest* bowling-ground in all Tartary."

[4] Almost given the stamp of truth to a *lie*. See *Twelfth Night*, page 46,
note 9.

[5] *Factionary* seems to be used here in its primitive sense ; *active*.

[6] *Virginal palms* of course means the palms or hands of virgins held up
in supplication.

this? No, you are deceived; therefore back to Rome, and prepare for your execution: you are condemn'd, our general has sworn you out of reprieve and pardon.

Men. Sirrah, if thy captain knew I were here, he would use me with estimation.

2 Sen. Come, my captain knows you not.

Men. I mean, thy general.

1 Sen. My general cares not for you. Back, I say, go; lest I let forth your half-pint of blood: back; that's the utmost of your having; back.

Men. Nay, but, fellow, fellow,—

Enter CORIOLANUS *and* AUFIDIUS.

Cor. What's the matter?

Men. Now, you companion, I'll say an errand for you: you shall now know that I am in estimation; you shall perceive that a Jack [7] guardant cannot office me from my son Coriolanus: guess, but by my entertainment with him, if thou stand'st not i' the state of hanging, or of some death more long in spectatorship, and crueller in suffering; behold now presently, and swoon for what's to come upon thee. —[*To* COR.] The glorious gods sit in hourly synod about thy particular prosperity, and love thee no worse than thy old father Menenius does! O my son, my son! thou art preparing fire for us; look thee, here's water to quench it. I was hardly moved to come to thee; but, being assured none but myself could move thee, I have been blown out of our gates with sighs; and conjure thee to pardon Rome, and thy petitionary countrymen. The good gods assuage

---

[7] Equivalent to *Jack in office*, one who is proud of his petty consequence. *Companion* was used as we use *fellow*.

thy wrath, and turn the dregs of it upon this varlet here, —
this, who, like a block, hath denied my access to thee.

   Cor. Away!

   Men. How! away!

   Cor. Wife, mother, child, I know not.   My affairs
Are servanted to others : though I owe
My revenge properly, my remission lies
In Volscian breasts.[8]   That we have been familiar,
Ingrate forgetfulness shall poison, rather
Than pity note how much.[9]   Therefore, be gone.
Mine ears against your suits are stronger than
Your gates against my force.   Yet, for I loved thee,
Take this along ; I writ it for thy sake,   *[Gives a letter.*
And would have sent it.   Another word, Menenius,
I will not hear thee speak. — This man, Aufidius,
Was my beloved in Rome : yet thou behold'st !

   Auf. You keep a constant temper.

             [Exeunt CORIOLANUS *and* AUFIDIUS.

   1 Sen. Now, sir, is your name Menenius?

   2 Sen. 'Tis a spell, you see, of much power : you know
the way home again.

   1 Sen. Do you hear how we are shent[10] for keeping your
greatness back?

   2 Sen. What cause do you think I have to swoon?

   Men. I neither care for the world nor your general : for
such things as you, I can scarce think there's any, ye're so
slight.   He that hath a will to die by himself[11] fears it not

---

[8] "Though my revenge is my own, or proper to myself, in the power of
forgiveness the Volscians are joined."   *Owe* for *own*, as usual.

[9] "Oblivious ingratitude shall *kill* our old friendship, rather than pity
shall give any sign how strong it was."

[10] *Shent* is an old word for *rebuked* or *scolded at*.

[11] That is, by his own hands.

from another: let your general do his worst. For you, be
that you are, long; and your misery increase with your age!
I say to you, as I was said to, Away!   [*Exit.*

1 Sen. A noble fellow, I warrant him.

2 Sen. The worthy fellow is our general: he's the rock,
the oak not to be wind-shaken.   [*Exeunt.*

SCENE III.— *The Tent of* CORIOLANUS.

Enter CORIOLANUS, AUFIDIUS, *and others.*

Cor. We will before the walls of Rome to-morrow
Set down our host. — My partner in this action,
You must report to th' Volscian lords, how plainly [1]
I have borne this business.

Auf.   Only their ends
You have respected; stopp'd your ears against
The general suit of Rome; never admitted
A private whisper, no, not with such friends
That thought them sure of you.

Cor.   This last old man,
Whom with a crack'd heart I have sent to Rome,
Loved me above the measure of a father;
Nay, godded me, indeed. Their latest refuge
Was to send him; for whose old love I have,
Though I show'd sourly to him, once more offer'd
The first conditions, which they did refuse,
And cannot now accept; to grace him only
That thought he could do more, a very little
I've yielded to: fresh embassies and suits,

---

1 *Plainly* is *openly;* remotely from artifice or concealment.

Nor from the State nor private friends, hereafter
Will I lend ear to. —   [*Shout within.*
                    Ha! what shout is this?
Shall I be tempted to infringe my vow
In the same time 'tis made? I will not. —

Enter, in mourning habits, VIRGILIA, VOLUMNIA, *leading
          young* MARCIUS, VALERIA, *and* Attendants.

My wife comes foremost; then the honour'd mould
Wherein this trunk was framed, and in her hand
The grandchild to her blood. — But out, affection!
All bond and privilege of nature, break!
Let it be virtuous to be obstinate. —
What is that curtsy worth? or those doves' eyes,
Which can make gods forsworn? I melt, and am not
Of stronger earth than others. My mother bows;
As if Olympus to a molehill should
In supplication nod; and my young boy
Hath an aspéct of intercession, which
Great Nature cries *Deny not.* Let the Volsces
Plough Rome, and harrow Italy: I'll never
Be such a gosling to obey instinct; but stand,
As if a man were author of himself,
And knew no other kin.
     Vir.   My lord and husband!
     Cor. These eyes are not the same I wore in Rome
     Vir. The sorrow that delivers us thus changed
Makes you think so.
     Cor.   Like a dull actor now,
I have forgot my part, and I am out,
Even to a full disgrace. — Best of my flesh,
Forgive my tyranny; but do not say,

For that, *Forgive our Romans*.   O, a kiss
Long as my exile, sweet as my revenge !
Now, by the jealous Queen of Heaven,[2] that kiss
I carried from thee, dear ; and my true lip
Hath virgin'd it e'er since. — You gods ! I prate,
And the most noble mother of the world
Leave unsaluted : sink, my knee, i' the earth ;   [*Kneels.*
Of thy deep duty more impression show
Than that of common sons.

   Vol. [*Raising him.*]   O, stand up bless'd !
Whilst, with no softer cushion than the flint,
I kneel before thee ; and unproperly
Show duty, as mistaken all this while
Between the child and parent.   [*Kneels.*

   Cor. [*Hastily raising her.*]   What is this ?
Your knees to me ? to your corrected son ?
Then let the pebbles on the angry beach
Fillip the stars ;[3] then let the mutinous winds
Strike the proud cedars 'gainst the fiery Sun ;
Murdering impossibility,[4] to make
What cannot be, slight work.

   Vol.   Thou art my warrior ;
I holp to frame thee.   Do you know this lady ?

   Cor. The noble sister of Publicola,

---

[2] Juno was the special guardian of marriage, and consequently the avenger of connubial perfidy.

[3] To *fillip* is to *thump* or *smite*. So that the image is of the enraged beach tossing or spitting the pebbles so high as to hit the stars ; — hyperbolical enough ! See *2 Henry IV.*, page 74, note 31. — We have a similar expression in *The Tempest*, i. 2: "The sea, mounting to th' welkin's cheek, dashes the fire out."

[4] Putting impossibility out of existence ; causing that there be no such thing.

The moon of Rome ; chaste as the icicle
That's curded by the frost from purest snow,
And hangs on Dian's temple.   Dear Valeria !
    Vol. This is a poor epitome of yours,
Which by th' interpretation [5] of full time
May show like all yourself.
    Cor.   The god of soldiers,
With the consent of súpreme Jove,[6] inform
Thy thoughts with nobleness ; that thou mayst prove
To shame unvulnerable, and stick i' the wars
Like a great sea-mark, standing every flaw,[7]
And saving those that eye thee !
    Vol.   Your knee, sirrah.
    Cor. That's my brave boy !
    Vol. Even he, your wife, this lady, and myself,
Are suitors to you.
    Cor.   I beseech you, peace :
Or, if you'd ask, remember this before,
The things I have forsworn to grant [8] may never
Be held by you denials.   Do not bid me
Dismiss my soldiers, or capitulate
Again with Rome's mechanics : tell me not
Wherein I seem unnatural ; desire not

---

[5] *Interpretation* is here equivalent to *development;* "which time will unfold into a complete, full-blown image of yourself."

[6] This is inserted with great decorum.   Jupiter was the tutelary god of Rome, and the Capitol was his temple.

[7] A *flaw* is a violent blast or sudden gust of wind.   Carew thus describes it, in his *Survey of Cornwall :* "One kind of these storms they call a *flaw,* or *flaugh,* which is a mighty gale of wind passing suddenly to the shore, and working strong effects upon whatsoever it encounters in its way."

[8] "Forsworn to grant" is sworn *not* to grant, and so forsworn, or perjured, *in* or *by granting*.   Still another instance of the infinitive used gerundively.

T' allay my rages and revenges with
Your colder reasons.

  Vol.   O, no more, no more !
You've said you will not grant us any thing ;
For we have nothing else to ask, but that
Which you deny already : yet we'll ask ;
That, if we fail in our request, the blame
May hang upon your hardness : therefore hear us.

  Cor. Aufidius, and you Volsces, mark ; for we'll
Hear nought from Rome in private. — Your request ?

  Vol. Should we be silent and not speak, our raiment
And state of bodies would bewray what life
We've led since thy exile. Think with thyself
How more unfortunate than all living women
Are we come hither ; since that thy sight, which should
Make our eyes flow with joy, hearts dance with comforts,
Constrains them weep, and shake with fear and sorrow ;
Making the mother, wife, and child, to see
The son, the husband, and the father, tearing
His country's bowels out. And to poor we
Thine enmity's most capital : thou barr'st us
Our prayers to the gods, which is a comfort
That all but we enjoy ; for how can we,
Alas, how can we for our country pray,
Whereto we're bound, together with thy victory,
Whereto we're bound ? alack, or we must lose
The country, our dear nurse, or else thy person,
Our comfort in the country. We must find
An evident calamity, though we had
Our wish, which side should win ; for either thou
Must, as a foreign recreant, be led
With manacles thorough our streets, or else

Triumphantly tread on thy country's ruin,
And bear the palm for having bravely shed
Thy wife and children's blood.   For myself, son,
I purpose not to wait on fortune till
These wars determine : if I cannot persuade thee
Rather to show a noble grace to both parts
Than seek the end of one, thou shalt no sooner
March to assault thy country than to tread —
Trust to't, thou shalt not — on thy mother's womb,
That brought thee to this world.

  Vir.   Ay, and on mine,
That brought you forth this boy, to keep your name
Living to time.

  Young Mar. 'A shall not tread on me :
I'll run away till I am bigger, then I'll fight.

  Cor. Not of a woman's tenderness to be,
Requires nor child nor woman's face to see.
I've sat too long.   [*Rising.*

  Vol.   Nay, go not from us thus.
If it were so that our request did tend
To save the Romans, thereby to destroy
The Volsces whom you serve, you might condemn us,
As poisonous of your honour : no ; our suit
Is, that you reconcile them : while the Volsces
May say, *This mercy we have show'd ;* the Romans,
This we received ; and each in either side
Give the all-hail to thee, and cry, *Be bless'd
For making up this peace !*   Thou know'st, great son,
The end of war's uncertain ; but this certain,
That, if thou conquer Rome, the benefit
Which thou shalt thereby reap is such a name,
Whose repetition will be dogg'd with curses ;

Whose chronicle thus writ : *The man was noble,*
But with his last attempt he wiped it out;
Destroy'd his country; and his name remains
To the ensuing age abhorr'd.   Speak to me, son :
Thou hast affected the fine strains of honour,
To imitate the graces of the gods ;
To tear with thunder the wide cheeks o' the air,
And yet to charge thy sulphur [9] with a bolt
That should but rive an oak. [10]   Why dost not speak?
Think'st thou it honourable for a noble man
Still to remember wrongs? — Daughter, speak you :
He cares not for your weeping. — Speak thou, boy ;
Perhaps thy childishness will move him more
Than can our reasons. — There's no man in the world
More bound to's mother ; yet here he lets me prate
Like one i' the stocks. — Thou'st never in thy life
Show'd thy dear mother any courtesy ;
When she, poor hen, fond of no second brood,
Has cluck'd thee to the wars, and safely home,
Loaden with honour.   Say my request's unjust,

[9] *Sulphur* is here put for *lightning;* the then unknown force that propelled the thunderbolt.   The idea is of Omnipotence, able to rend the universe in pieces, yet satisfied to charge its thunder-engines with a bolt that only splits an oak.

[10] A very high and noble image or expression of character ; but perhaps the grandeur of the image somewhat obscures the sense.   The "fine strains of honour" intended are such as have their life in strength married to gentleness, or in a contempt of danger and death united with a tender and pitiful heart.   The idea was evidently a favourite one with Shakespeare ; and many of his noblest strains of pathos turn upon a style of manhood which fears not power, but whose soul-storm falters into music at the touch of compassion. The author of *Ecce Homo* aptly quotes this passage as illustrating how "the noblest and most amiable thing is power mixed with gentleness, the reposing, self-restraining attitude of strength."   Such graces are indeed Divine.   See *The Merchant*, page 169, note 33.

And spurn me back : but, if it be not so,
Thou art not honest ; and the gods will plague thee,
That thou restrain'st from me the duty which
To a mother's part belongs. — He turns away :
Down, ladies ; let us shame him with our knees.
To his surname *Coriolanus* 'longs more pride
Than pity to our prayers.   Down ; an end ;
This is the last : so we will home to Rome,
And die among our neighbours. — Nay, behold's :
This boy, that cannot tell what he would have,
But kneels and holds up hands for fellowship,
Does reason our petition with more strength
Than thou hast to deny't. — Come, let us go :
This fellow had a Volscian to his mother ;
His wife is in Corioli, and this child
Like him by chance.[11] — Yet give us our dispatch :
I'm hush'd until our city be a-fire,
And then I'll speak a little.
       Cor. [*After holding her by the hand in silence.*] O mother,
            mother !
What have you done?   Behold, the heavens do ope,
The gods look down, and this unnatural scene
They laugh at.   O my mother, mother !   O !
You've won a happy victory to Rome ;
But for your son, — believe it, O, believe it, —
Most dangerously you have with him prevail'd,
If not most mortal to him.   But, let it come. —
Aufidius, though I cannot make true wars,
I'll frame convenient peace.   Now, good Aufidius,
Were you in my stead, say, would you have heard

---

[11] This child is not indeed his son, but only *happens* to resemble him.

A mother less? or granted less, Aufidius?

Auf. I was moved withal.

Cor.   I dare be sworn you were:
And, sir, it is no little thing to make
Mine eyes to sweat compassion. But, good sir,
What peace you'll make, advise me: for my part,
I'll not to Rome, I'll back with you; and pray you,
Stand to me in this cause. — O mother! wife!

Auf. [*Aside.*] I'm glad thou'st set thy mercy and thy
    honour
At difference in thee: out of that I'll work
Myself a firmer fortune. [*The* Ladies *make signs to* CORIO.

Cor. [*To the* Ladies.] Ay, by-and-by:
We will but drink together;[12] and you shall bear
A better witness back than words, which we,
On like conditions, will have counter-seal'd.
Come, enter with us. Ladies, you deserve
To have a temple built you: all the swords
In Italy, and her confederate arms,
Could not have made this peace.   [*Exeunt.*

SCENE IV. — *Rome.   A public Place.*

Enter MENENIUS *with* SICINIUS.

Men. See you yond coign o' the Capitol, yond corner-
stone?

Sic. Why, what of that?

Men. If it be possible for you to displace it with your
little finger, there is some hope the ladies of Rome, especially

---

[12] Meaning, apparently, that Aufidius, or the Volscian leaders, and himself will but delay long enough for an amicable pledge.

his mother, may prevail with him.   But I say there is no hope in't : our throats are sentenced, and stay upon[1] execution.

Sic. Is't possible that so short a time can alter the condition[2] of a man?

Men. There is difference between a grub and a butterfly ; yet your butterfly was a grub.   This Marcius is grown from man to dragon : he has wings ; he's more than a creeping thing.

Sic. He loved his mother dearly.

Men. So did he me ; and he no more remembers his mother now than an eight-year-old horse.   The tartness of his face sours ripe grapes : when he walks, he moves like an engine, and the ground shrinks before his treading : he is able to pierce a corslet with his eye ; talks like a knell, and his hum is a battery.   He sits in his state, as a thing made for Alexander.[3]   What he bids be done, is finish'd with his bidding.   He wants nothing of a god but eternity, and a heaven to throne in.

Sic. Yes, mercy, if you report him truly.

Men. I paint him in the character.   Mark what mercy his mother shall bring from him : there is no more mercy in him than there is milk in a male tiger ; that shall our poor city find ; and all this is 'long of you.[4]

Sic. The gods be good unto us !

Men. No, in such a case the gods will not be good unto us.   When we banish'd him, we respected not them ; and, he returning to break our necks, they respect not us.

Enter a Messenger.

---

[1] To *stay upon* means the same as to *wait for*.
[2] *Condition*, here, as usual, is *temper* or *disposition*.
[3] That is, like an image made in the likeness of Alexander.
[4] "*Along* of you " is *because* of you.   So the phrase occurs repeatedly.

Mess. Sir, if you'd save your life, fly to your house:
The plébeians have got your fellow-tribune,
And hale him up and down; all swearing, if
The Roman ladies bring not comfort home,
They'll give him death by inches.

Enter a second Messenger.

Sic.   What's the news?
   2 Mess. Good news, good news! the ladies have pre-
     vail'd,
The Volscians are dislodged, and Marcius gone:
A merrier day did never yet greet Rome,
No, not th' expulsion of the Tarquins.
   Sic.   Friend,
Art certain this is true?
   2 Mess.   Ay, sir, most certain, —
As certain as I know the Sun is fire:
Where have you lurk'd, that you make doubt of it?
Ne'er through an arch so hurried the blown tide
As the recomforted through th' gates.   Why, hark you!
    [*Trumpets and hautboys sounded, and drums beaten,*
            all together; shouting also, within.
The trumpets, sackbuts, psalteries, and fifes,
Tabors, and cymbals, and the shouting Romans,
Make the Sun dance.   Hark you!   [*Shouting again within.*
   Men.   This is good news:
I will go meet the ladies.   This Volumnia
Is worth of Consuls, Senators, patricians,
A city full; of tribunes, such as you,
A sea and land full.   You've pray'd well to-day:
This morning for ten thousand of your throats
I'd not have given a doit.   Hark, how they joy!
         [*Shouting and music still, within.*

Sic. First, the gods bless you for your tidings ; next,
Accept my thankfulness.

2 Mess. Sir, we have all
Great cause to give great thanks.

Sic. They're near the city?

2 Mess. Almost at point to enter.

Sic. We will meet them,
And help the joy. [*Exeunt.*

SCENE V. — *The Same. A Street near the Gate.*

Enter in procession, VOLUMNIA, VIRGILIA, VALERIA, *&c., accompanied by* Senators, Patricians, *and* Citizens.

1 Sen. Behold our patroness, the life of Rome !
Call all your tribes together, praise the gods,
And make triumphant fires ; strew flowers before them :
Unshout the noise that banish'd Marcius,
Repeal him with the welcome of his mother ;
Cry, *Welcome, ladies, welcome !*

All. Welcome, ladies,
Welcome ! [*A flourish with drums and trumpets. Exeunt.*

SCENE VI. — *Corioli. A public Place.*

Enter AUFIDIUS, *with* Attendants.

Auf. Go tell the lords o' the city I am here ;
Deliver them this paper : having read it,
Bid them repair to th' market-place ; where I,
Even in theirs and in the commons' ears,
Will vouch the truth of it. Him I accuse
The city ports by this hath enter'd, and

Intends t' appear before the people, hoping
To purge himself with words : dispatch. —

        [*Exeunt* Attendants.

 Enter three or four Conspirators *of* AUFIDIUS's *faction.*

          Most welcome !

 1 Con. How is it with our general?
 Auf.   Even so
As with a man by his own alms empoison'd,
And with his charity slain.
 2 Con.   Most noble sir,
If you do hold the same intent wherein
You wish'd us parties, we'll deliver you
Of your great danger.
 Auf.   Sir, I cannot tell :
We must proceed as we do find the people.
 3 Con. The people will remain uncertain whilst
'Twixt you there's difference ; but the fall of either
Makes the survivor heir of all.
 Auf.   I know it ;
And my pretext to strike at him admits
A good construction. I raised him, and I pawn'd
Mine honour for his truth : who being so heighten'd,
He water'd his new plants with dews of flattery,
Seducing so my friends ; and, to this end,
He bow'd his nature, never known before
But to be rough, unswayable, and fierce.
 3 Con. Sir, his stoutness
When he did stand for Consul, which he lost
By lack of stooping, —
 Auf.   That I would have spoke of.
Being banish'd for't, he came unto my hearth ;

Presented to my knife his throat : I took him ;
Made him joint-servant with me ; gave him way
In all his own desires ; nay, let him choose
Out of my files, his projects to accomplish,
My best and freshest men ; served his designments
In mine own person ; holp to reap the fame
Which he did end all his ;[1] and took some pride
To do myself this wrong : till, at the last,
I seem'd his follower, not partner ; and
He waged me with his countenance,[2] as if
I had been merçenary.

   1 Con.   So he did, my lord ;
The army marvell'd at it ; and, in the last,
When he had carried Rome, and that we look'd
For no less spoil than glory, —

   Auf.   There was it ;
For which my sinews shall be stretch'd upon him.
At a few drops of women's rheum, which are
As cheap as lies, he sold the blood and labour
Of our great action : therefore shall he die,
And I'll renew me in his fall.   But, hark !

[*Drums and trumpets sound, with great shouts of the people.*

---

[1] It appears that *end* was and still is a technical term for the finishing of
harvest-work.   The Rev. Mr. Arrowsmith has produced, from recent adver-
tisements in Gloucestershire, the phrases " well-*ended* wheat ricks " and "a
rick of well-*ended* hay " ; meaning, apparently, stacks of wheat well stored
&c.   So that the meaning of the text is, that Coriolanus had managed to
appropriate for his own exclusive use the whole harvest of renown which
Aufidius had helped to gather and prepare.

[2] The sense of to *wage*, as here used, still lives in *wages*.   So in Heywood's *Wise Woman of Hogsdon* : " I receive thee gladly to my house, and
wage thy stay."   The meaning in the text is, " He treated me as his depen-
dent or hireling, and paid me with bland looks and patronizing airs, as a
kind of wages."   Or *countenance*, here, as in at least two other places, may
mean *entertainment* or *reception*.   See *As You Like It*, page 30, note 4.

1 Con. Your native town you enter'd like a post,
And had no welcomes home ; but he returns,
Splitting the air with noise.

2 Con.   And patient fools,
Whose children he hath slain, their base throats tear
With giving him glory.

3 Con.   Therefore, at your vantage,
Ere he express himself, or move the people
With what he would say, let him feel your sword,
Which we will second.   When he lies along,
After your way his tale pronounced shall bury
His reasons with his body.

Auf.   Say no more :
Here come the lords.

Enter the Lords *of the City.*

Lords. You are most welcome home.

Auf.   I've not deserved it.
But, worthy lords, have you with heed perused
What I have written to you?

Lords.   We have.

1 Lord.   And grieve to hear't.
What faults he made before the last, I think
Might have found easy fines ; but, there to end
Where he was to begin, and give away
The benefit of our levies, answering us
With our own charge,[3] making a treaty where
There was a yielding, — this admits no excuse.

Auf. He approaches : you shall hear him.

---

[3] " Instead of spoils and victory, presenting the bill, — for ourselves to
pay."

Enter CORIOLANUS, *with drum and colours ; a crowd of* Citizens *with him.*

  Cor. Hail, lords ! I am return'd your soldier ;
No more infected with my country's love
Than when I parted hence, but still subsisting
Under your great command. You are to know,
That prosperously I have attempted, and,
With bloody passage, led your wars even to
The gates of Rome. Our spoils we have brought home
Do more than counterpoise a full third part
The charges of the action. We've made peace,
With no less honour to the Antiates
Than shame to th' Romans ; and we here deliver,
Subscribed by th' Consuls and patricians,
Together with the seal o' the Senate, what
We have compounded on.
  Auf.   Read it not, noble lords ;
But tell the traitor, in the high'st degree
He hath abused your powers.
  Cor. Traitor ! how now !
  Auf.   Ay, traitor, Marcius !
  Cor.   Marcius !
  Auf. Ay, Marcius, Caius Marcius : dost thou think
I'll grace thee with that robbery, thy stol'n name
Coriolanus, in Corioli ? —
You lords and heads o' the State, perfidiously
He has betray'd your business, and given up,
For certain drops of salt, your city Rome —
I say, your city — to his wife and mother ;
Breaking his oath and resolution, like
A twist of rotten silk ; never admitting

Counsel o' the war ; but at his nurse's tears
He whined and roar'd away your victory ;
That pages blush'd at him, and men of heart
Look'd wondering each at other.

  Cor.   Hear'st thou, Mars ?

  Auf. Name not the god, thou boy of tears !

  Cor.   Ha !

  Auf. No more.[4]

  Cor. Measureless liar, thou hast made my heart
Too great for what contains it. *Boy !* O slave ! —
Pardon me, lords, 'tis the first time that ever
I was forced to scold. Your judgments, my grave lords,
Must give this cur the lie : and his own notion[5] —
Who wears my stripes impress'd upon him ; that
Must bear my beating to his grave — shall join
To thrust the lie unto him.

  1 Lord. Peace, both, and hear me speak.

  Cor. Cut me to pieces, Volsces ! men and lads,
Stain all your edges on me ! — *Boy !* false hound !
If you have writ your annals true, 'tis there,
That, like an eagle in a dove-cote, I
Flutter'd your Volscians in Corioli ;
Alone I did it. *Boy !*

  Auf.   Why, noble lords,
Will you be put in mind of his blind fortune,
Which was your shame, by this unholy braggart,
'Fore your own eyes and ears ?

  All the Conspirators. Let him die for't !

  Citizens. Tear him to pieces ! — Do it presently ! — He

---

 [4] No more than a boy of tears.

 [5] *Notion*, as the context shows, is here equivalent to *judgment*. Repeatedly so. See *Macbeth*, page 101, note 16.

kill'd . my son ! — My daughter ! — He kill'd my cousin
Marcus ! — He kill'd my father ! —

2 Lord. Peace, ho ! — no outrage ; — peace !
The man is noble, and his fame folds-in
This orb o' the Earth.[6]   His last offences to us
Shall have judicious [7] hearing. — Stand, Aufidius,
And trouble not the peace.

Cor.   O, that I had him,
With six Aufidiuses, or more, his tribe,
To use my lawful sword !

Auf.   Insolent villain !

All the Conspirators. Kill, kill, kill, kill, kill him !

[AUFIDIUS *and the* Conspirators *draw, and kill* CORIO-
LANUS, *who falls :* AUFIDIUS *stands on him.*

Lords.   Hold, hold, hold, hold !

Auf. My noble masters, hear me speak.

1 Lord.   O Tullus, —

2 Lord. Thou'st done a deed whereat valour will weep.

3 Lord. Tread not upon him. — Masters all, be quiet ;
Put up your swords.

Auf. My lords, when you shall know — as in this rage,
Provoked by him, you cannot — the great danger
Which this man's life did owe [8] you, you'll rejoice
That he is thus cut off.   Please it your Honours
To call me to your Senate, I'll deliver

---

[6] His fame overspreads the world.

[7] *Judicious* here has the sense of *judicial ;* the two being formerly con-
vertible terms.

[8] To speak of *owing* you danger sounds odd, nor do I remember another
instance of the word used in exactly the same way. The meaning clearly is,
to *have*, to *threaten*, or be *fraught with* danger to you. Perhaps the phrase,
still common, " He owes me a grudge," that is, he has a grudge against me,
is of similar origin.

Myself your loyal servant, or endure
Your heaviest censure.

   1 Lord.   Bear from hence his body,
And mourn you for him ; let him be regarded
As the most noble corse that ever herald
Did follow to his urn.

   2 Lord.   His own impatience
Takes from Aufidius a great part of blame.
Let's make the best of it.

   Auf.   My rage is gone ;
And I am struck with sorrow. — Take him up ; —
Help, three o' the chiefest soldiers ; I'll be one. —
Beat thou the drum, that it speak mournfully :
Trail your steel pikes. — Though in this city he
Hath widow'd and unchilded many a one,
Which to this hour bewail the injury,
Yet he shall have a noble memory.[9] —
Assist.

                 [Exeunt, bearing the body of CORIOLANUS.
                           A dead march sounded.

   [9] *Memory,* again, for *memorial* or *monument.*   See page 165, note 3.

CRITICAL NOTES.

—◆—

ACT I., SCENE I.

Page 38. *1 Cit. Against him first.* — In the original, this speech has the prefix "*All*," just as have the preceding speeches to which "*Citizens*" is prefixed in the text. Malone thought it should be assigned to *1 Citizen*, and surely he was right.

P. 38. *2 Cit. Nay, but speak not maliciously.* — The original prefixes "*All*" to this speech. Evidently wrong, as the second Citizen endeavours, all through this scene, to assuage the wrath of his fellows.

P. 39. *He did it to please his mother, and* partly to be *proud.* — So Hanmer. The old text reads "and *to be partly* proud." Capell prints *partly* before "to please his mother." Staunton thinks it should be *portly;* Lettsom, *pertly,* meaning *openly, clearly.*

P. 39. *1 Cit. Our business is not unknown to the Senate;* &c. — In the original, this speech is given to the second *Citizen,* as are also the subsequent speeches of this scene which are here assigned to the first *Citizen.* This is clearly wrong, as it is quite at odds with the course of the preceding dialogue The second *Citizen* is a temperate defender of the hero. Capell made the correction.

P. 40. *Care for us! True, indeed, they ne'er cared for us yet.* — So the old copies. Several modern editions print "True, indeed! They ne'er cared for us yet."

P. 40. *But, since it serves my purpose, I will venture To stale't a little more.* — The original has *scale* instead of *stale.* The forced attempts made to justify *scale* are, I think, a full condemnation of it. Corrected by Theobald.

P. 41. *And, mutually* participant, *did minister,* &c. — The original has "And mutually *participate.*"

P. 44. *He that will give good words to* ye *will flatter*
      Beneath abhorring. — The original has *thee* instead of *ye.* The old abbreviations of the two words were often confounded. Here the context imperatively requires *ye.* Corrected by Dyce.

P. 44. *And hew down oaks with rushes.* Trust *ye?* Hang *ye!* — The original reads "*Hang* ye: *trust ye?*" The transposition was proposed by Coleridge, and is approved by Walker.

P. 44. *With every minute you do change* your *mind.* — So Collier's second folio. The old text has "change *a* mind."

P. 46. *Five tribunes to defend their vulgar wisdoms,*
      Of their own choice: one's Junius Brutus, one
      Sicinius Velutus, &c. — So Walker. The old text lacks *one* after *Brutus.* The insertion is, I think, fairly called for by both sense and metre.

P. 46. *The rabble should have first* unroof'd *the city.* — The original has *unroo'st.* Theobald's correction.

P. 48. *The present* war *devour him!* — The old text has *Warres.*

ACT I., SCENE 2.

P. 51. *Let us alone to guard* Corioli. — Here, and throughout the play, the original has *Corioles,* or *Carioles.*

P. 51. *If they set down before's, for their remove*
      Bring up your army. — The original has *the* instead of *their,* which was proposed by Johnson.

ACT I., SCENE 3.

P. 52. I *see him pluck Aufidius down by th' hair.* The original omits *I.* Supplied by Rowe.

P. 53. *Than Hector's forehead when it spit forth blood*
    At Grecian swords, contemning. — *Tell Valeria,* &c. — The original reads " At Grecian *sword. Contenning,* tell *Valeria* " ; the second folio, " At Grecian *swordes Conténding :* tell," &c. Collier's second folio has *contemning.* Lettsom proposed "*As* Grecian swords contemning."

P. 54. *Catch'd it again :* and, *whether his fall enraged him, or how 'twas, he did so set his teeth,* &c. — So Hanmer. The original has *or* instead of *and.*

ACT I., SCENE 4.

P. 56. *No, nor a man that fears you* more *than he ;*
    That's lesser than a little. — Instead of *more,* the original has *less,* which directly contradicts the sense of the passage. Both Johnson and Capell proposed *more.*

P. 57. *You shames of Rome ! you herd of* — *Boils and plagues*
    Plaster you o'er : &c. — The original reads " you *Heard* of *Byles* and Plagues." The correction is Johnson's, and the reading aptly marks the speaker's explosive rage. Collier's second folio has " *unheard* of Byles," &c. ; which Dyce seems to think very well of, though he does not adopt it. I am by no means sure that it ought not to be preferred.

P. 57. *If you'll stand fast, we'll beat them to their wives,*
    As they us to our trenches. Follow me. — Instead of *Follow me,* the original has, simply, *followes.* The reading in the text is Lettsom's ; a very valuable correction.

P. 58. *Who,* sensible, *outdares his senseless sword,*
    And, when it bows, stands *up.* — *Thou art* lost, *Marcius.* — In the first of these lines, the original reads " Who *sensibly* out-dares." In the second, it has *stand'st* instead of *stands,* and *left* instead of *lost.* The latter correction is Collier's. Thirlby changed *sensibly* to *sensible.*

P. 58.   *Thou wast a soldier*
    Even to Cato's *wish.* — The original has " to *Calves* wish." Corrected by Theobald. See foot-note 7.

ACT I., SCENE 5.

P. 59. *See here these movers that do prize their* hours
At a crack'd drachma. — Pope and Johnson changed *hours* to *honours*. The former is ascertained to be the right reading, by referring to the authority which the Poet followed: "The city being taken in this sort, the most part of the souldiers began incontinently to spoile, to cary away, and to looke up the bootie they had wonne. But Martius was marvellous angry with them, and cryed out on them, that it was no time now to looke after spoile, and runne stragling here and there to enrich themselves." — I must add that the original has *Drachme*. Collier, White, and Dyce print *drachm;* Staunton *dram;* I cannot tell why. Metre requires a dissyllable.

P. 60.   *Now the fair goddess, Fortune,*
Fall deep in love with thee; and her great charms
Misguide th' *opposers' swords.* — So Walker. The old text has "Misguide *thy* Opposers swords."

ACT I., SCENE 6.

P. 61.   Ye *Roman gods,*
Lead their successes as we wish our own, &c. — The original has *The* instead of *Ye.* Hanmer's correction.

P. 62. *More than I know the sound of Marcius' tongue*
From every meaner man's. — The original has *man* instead of *man's.* Corrected by Hanmer.

P. 63. *Will the time serve to tell? I do not think* so.
Where is the enemy? — So Lettsom. The original lacks *so.* Collier's second folio reads "think *it.*"

P. 64. Go we along; *make you a sword of me.*
If these shows be not outward, &c. — The original reads, "*Oh me alone,* make you a sword of me," &c. This is commonly printed "O me, alone! make you a sword of **me?**" &c. Dyce, however, prints

"O, me alone!" &c. No one seems able to make any sense out of the old text, however punctuated. Heath says, "This is undoubtedly nonsense. I conceive we should read '*Let* me alone ; make you a sword of me'?" But I cannot make this reading cohere with the context. Singer prints "*Come! along!* make you a sword of me." The reading in the text is suggested by Mr. R. Whitelaw, in the "Rugby edition" of the play. It gives about the same meaning as Singer's, and is, I think, more in the Poet's manner. That meaning is, of course, "Let us proceed to the work ; use me as your sword" ; and, as they already have the speaker in their arms, the language is not strained. We have repeated instances of *me* and *we* confounded, and also of *along* misprinted *alone*.

P. 64.   *A certain number,*
     Though thanks to all, must I select : the rest
     Shall bear the business in some other fight. — The original reads "must I select *from all :* The rest," &c. The words *from all* are re-dundant in metre, and, I think, much worse than redundant in sense. Probably interpolated for the sake of the jingle. Hanmer omits them.

P. 64.   *Please you to march ;*
     And I shall quickly draw out my command, &c. — The old text reads "And *foure* shall quickly draw." I cannot imagine — it seems that nobody can — what business *four* has there. Singer substitutes *some*, which is better than *four* indeed, but far from satisfactory. Lett-som proposes *we*, meaning the speaker and Cominius ; and he observes that "*four* may have been derived from the sixth line above." This is certainly better than *some ;* still I prefer *I*, which was proposed by Capell.

ACT I., SCENE 8.

P. 66. *Not Afric owns a serpent I abhor*
     More than thy fame I envy. — The original reads "More than thy fame *and* envy." The construction commonly put upon the pas-sage is, "Not Afric owns a serpent that I more abhor and envy than I do thy fame" ; *envy* being interpreted in the old sense of *hate*. But why should Aufidius profess to abhor and hate the *fame* of Marcius ?

when the plain truth is, that he *desires* or *covets* his fame, and therefore *envies* him the possession of it. The theory of the change is, that the pronoun *I* was mistaken by the printer for the usual contraction of *and.* The correction is from Collier's second folio.

ACT I., SCENE 9.

> P. 68.   *May these same instruments, which you profane,*
> > *Never sound more !*   Shall *drums and trumpets,* when
> > *I' the field, prove flatterers ?   Let Courts and cities be*
> > *Made all of false-faced soothing,* where *steel grows*
> > *Soft as the parasite's silk : let* them *be made*
> > *An overture for th' wars.* — This is one of the most trouble-
some passages in the very troublesome text of this play. In the second and third lines, the original reads "*When* drums and trumpets *shall* i' the field prove flatterers, let courts," &c. The transposition of *when* and *shall,* so as to make the clause interrogative, was proposed by Singer. I think it removes the worst of the difficulty. In the fourth line, the original has *when* instead of *where ;* an easy and common misprint. In the fifth line also, the original reads "let *him* be made," &c.; where *him* can hardly be reconciled with any possible explana-tion of the passage. Every one experienced in proof-reading knows how apt *him* and *them* or *'em* are to be misprinted for each other ; and in fact the originals of Shakespeare have divers instances of such mis-printing. As the text is here printed *them* refers to "drums and trum-pets." Dyce, following Collier's second folio, changes *An overture* to *A coverture,* understanding it to mean *covering,* that is *armour.* But I question whether *coverture* was ever used in that sense. Shakespeare has the word in two places, and in both it bears a sense very different from that ; as "couchèd in the woodbine *coverture,*" and "in night's *coverture* we may surprise and take him." *Overture* is *introduction* or *prelude.* I add an exact transcript of the old text :

> > May these same Instruments, which you prophane,
> > Never sound more: *when* Drums and Trumpets *shall*
> > I' th' field prove flatterers, let Courts and Cities be
> > Made all of false-fac'd soothing:
> > *When* Steele growes soft, as the Parasites Silke,
> > Let *him* be made an Overture for th' Warres.

P. 69. CAIUS MARCIUS CORIOLANUS. — *Bear*
Th' addition nobly ever ! — Both here and in the next speech,
the original has " *Marcius Caius Coriolanus.*"

ACT I., SCENE 10.

P. 72.   *My* valour, *poison'd*
With only suffering stain by him, for him,
Shall fly out of itself.—The original reads " my *valors* poison'd,"
&c. The misprinting of plurals and singulars for each other is one of
the commonest. The correction is Pope's.

P. 72. *The prayers of priests nor times of sacrifice,*
Embankments *all of fury,* &c. — The original has *Embarque-*
ments. Hanmer changed this to *Embankments,* which Walker says "is
the true reading."

ACT II., SCENE I.

P. 75. *Said to be something imperfect in favouring the* thirst *com-*
plaint. — The original reads " *first* complaint " ; in which there
appears neither humour nor sense. *Thirst* is derived from Collier's
second folio. There can be little hesitation in receiving it, as it
makes both the sense and the humour perfect. Lettsom thinks it should
be *first complainer,* and that the clause should come in after "forehead of the morning."

P. 75. *I* cannot *say your Worships have deliver'd the matter well,*
&c. — The original reads " I *can* say " ; a palpable error.

P. 75. *Yet they lie deadly that tell you* you *have good faces.* — The
original lacks the second *you;* another palpable error.

P. 75. *What harm can your* bisson *conspetuities glean out of this*
character, &c. — The original has *beesome,* doubtless a misprint for
bisson, which is an old word for *blind,* and which was formerly spelt in
various ways. In a later scene we have, apparently, the same word
misprinted *bosome.* See foot-note 8.

P. 77. *The most sovereign prescription in Galen is but* empiricutic, &c. — The original has *Emperickqutique*, for which Collier's second folio substitutes *empiric physic*. See foot-note 13.

P. 79.   *Where he hath won,*
        With fame, a name to Caius Marcius ; these
        In honour follows Coriolanus. — Welcome,
        Welcome to Rome, renown'd Coriolanus! — Here, again, the original transposes the names, *Martius Caius*, and also repeats them before *Coriolanus* in the next line. The first *welcome* is wanting in the old text. The insertion is Walker's.

P. 81. *From whom I have received not only greetings,*
        But with them charge *of honours.* — So Theobald and Collier's second folio. The original has *change* instead of *charge*.

P. 83. *He cannot temperately transport his honours*
        From where he should begin to th' *end; &c.* — The original has " begin *and* end." I have tried in vain to make any sense out of this reading ; and the strained yet futile attempts which have been made at explaining it are to me strong argument of its being wrong ; for by the same methods almost any words may be made to yield almost any sense. Another reading has occurred to me, " '*Tween* where he should begin and end." This would give the same sense, or nearly the same, as the reading in the text. And as the capitals *F* and *T* are commonly written, either might easily be mistaken for the other ; under which mistake the rest of the word would naturally be assimilated accordingly. — Since writing the above, I find that " begin *to th'* end " was proposed by Seymour. See note on "And for the gap," &c., *Cymbeline*, page 209.

P. 83. *That he will give them, make as little question*
        As he is proud to do't. — So Reed, 1803. The original has " make *I* as little question " ; which is against both sense and metre ; *make* being clearly in the same construction as *doubt not*, fourth line above. Lettsom approves the omission.

P. 84. *Of no more soul nor fitness for the world*
        Than camels in the *war.* — So Hanmer. The original has " in *their* war."

P. 84.   *This, as you say, suggested*
  At some time when his soaring insolence
  Shall touch *the people, will be* as *fire*
  To kindle their dry stubble. — The original has *teach* instead of *touch*, and "be *his* fire." The former correction is Hanmer's, the latter Capell's. Pope reads "be *the* fire."

ACT II., SCENE 2.

P. 85. *If he did not care whether he had their love or no,* he'd *waved indifferently 'twixt,* &c. — The original has "*he* waved." The slight change here made is Lettsom's. Of course the meaning is, "he *would have* waved."

P. 86. *Bonneted* into their estimation and report, *without any further deed to have them at all.* — The old text reads "bonneted, without any further deed, to have them at all *into their estimation, and report.*" Pope altered *have* to *heave*, which has been generaly adopted, though it necessitates a forced and very questionable explanation of *bonneted*. The right construction is, I think, clearly that given in the text; but it is, to say the least, not easy to get the sense of that construction from the old order of the words. Nor is the transposition which I have made a whit more free or bold than a great many others that are commonly thought needful, as indeed most of them are. See foot-note 2.

P. 87. *By Caius Marcius Coriolanus ; whom*
  We meet *here, both to thank,* &c. — Here, again, the original transposes the names, *Martius Caius*, and also has *met* instead of *meet*.

P. 89. *He had rather venture all his limbs for honour*
  Than one on's *ears to hear't.* — The original has "Then *on ones* Eares."

P. 89. *When with his Amazonian* chin he *drove,* &c. — The original has *Shinne* instead of *chin*.

P. 90.   *As* waves *before*
    A vessel under sail, so men obey'd,
        And fell below his stem. — So the second folio ; the first has *weeds* instead of *waves.* Singer aptly remarks, that " a vessel *stemming the waves* is an image much more suitable to the prowess of Coriolanus than the displacing of weeds." Lettsom also prefers *waves ;* and observes, that " the sense requires a circumstance that happens usually, *not exceptionally,* to ships under sail."

ACT II., SCENE 3.

P. 96. *You know the cause,* sirs, *of my standing here.* — The original has *Sir* instead of *sirs.* As the speaker is addressing the " brace " of citizens who have just entered, *sirs* is clearly right. Probably misprinted from having *sir* directly under it in the next line. Corrected by Rowe.

P. 96. *Ay,* not *mine own desire.* — So the third folio. The earlier editions have *but* and *no* instead of *not.*

P. 98. *Why in this* woolvish toge *should I stand here,* &c. — The original has *Woolvish tongue ;* the second folio, *gowne* instead of *tongue,* which is doubtless a misprint for *toge.* For *woolvish* Collier's second folio substitutes *woolless,* which Dyce adopts. As the toga was always made of wool, I doubt whether the Poet would have called it *woolless.* See foot-note 9.

P. 98.   *Battles thrice six*
    I've seen, and heard of ; *for your voices have*
    Done many things ; &c. — The words " and *heard of* " seem, to say the least, rather odd and out of place. Perhaps it should be " and *shared of* " ; which is a modest equivalent for " *been a part* of," and is good English for " *had a share* of " : therewithal it accords with what Cominius says in the preceding scene ; where, after describing the hero's first exploit, he continues, " And in the brunt of *seventeen* battles since," &c. Farmer proposed to read " battles thrice six I've seen, and *you have* heard of." See, however, foot-note 11.

P. 99. *May I*, then, *change these garments ?* — So Hamner. The original lacks *then*.

P. 100.   *To my poor unworthy* notion,
          He mock'd us when he begg'd our voices. — So Walker. The old text has *notice* instead of *notion*. Here, as in divers other places, *notion* is equivalent to *understanding* or *judgment*.

P. 102. *Than dogs, that are as often beat for barking*
          As they are *kept to do so.* — Instead of *they are*, the original has *therefore*, which makes an ugly tautology with *to do so*.

P. 102.   *Took from you*
          The apprehension of his present portance,
          Which, gibing most *ungravely, he did fashion*
          After th' inveterate hate he bears you. — The original reads "Which *most gibingly,* ungravely," &c. ; a breach of metrical order quite unusual with the Poet. The reading in the text was proposed by Lettsom. White transfers *Which* to the end of the preceding line, and thus disorders the metre of that line.

P. 103. *Of the same House Publius and Quintus were,*
          That our best water brought by conduits hither ;
          And Censorinus, who was *nobly named so,*
          Twice being chosen *censor* by the people,
          Was his great ancestor. — Instead of the third and fourth of these lines, the original has merely "And Nobly nam'd so, twice being Censor." So that, in effect, a whole line has to be supplied in order to make any sense of the passage. The words supplied are in accordance with the narration in Plutarch, from whence this passage is taken : "The house of the Martians at Rome was of the number of the patricians, out of which hath sprong many noble personages, whereof Ancus Martius was one, King Numaes daughter's sonne, who was king of Rome after Tullus Hostilius. Of the *same house* were Publius and Quintus, who brought to Rome their best water they had by conduits. Censorinus *came of that familie,* that was so surnamed because the people had chosen him censor twice." Publius and Quintus and Censorinus were not the ancestors of Coriolanus, but his descendants. Caius Marcius Rutilius did not obtain the name of Censorinus till the

year of Rome 487; and the Marcian waters were not brought to the city by aqueducts till near 350 years after the death of Coriolanus. Shakespeare confounded the ancestors and posterity of Coriolanus together.

ACT III., SCENE I.

P. 106. *Hath he not pass'd the* nobles *and the* commons? — So Rowe. The original has "the *Noble* and the *Common*." The second folio changes *Common* to *Commons*, but leaves *Noble* unchanged. Evidently both should be changed or neither.

P. 109.   *O good, but most unwise patricians! why,*
          You grave, but reckless Senators, have you thus
          Given Hydra here *to choose an officer,*
          That with his peremptory shall, *being but*
          The horn and noise o' the monster, &c. — In the first of these lines, the original has "O *God!* but most unwise Patricians:" &c. We have other clear instances of *God* misprinted for *good.* — In the third line, Dyce substitutes *heart* for *here;* very infelicitously, as I cannot but think. For the patricians have not given the people the *heart,* that is, the disposition or spirit, to choose Tribunes; the people had that before; but they have granted to them the *legal power* or *right;* have given their consent to such a law. Coriolanus regards the common people *everywhere* as a many-headed monster, like the Hydra; and what he is now complaining of is, that *here,* in Rome, this monster is allowed to choose a special officer who can do such and such things. As for the passages quoted by Dyce in support of his change, I can but say that they seem to me quite irrelevant. See foot-note 12. — In the fifth line, again, the old text has *monsters* instead of *monster.* As the word evidently refers to *Hydra* a little before, there can be no doubt, I think, that it should be in the singular. Corrected by Capell, and in Collier's second folio.

P. 110.   *If* they *have power,*
          Let them have cushions by you; if none, revoke
          Your dangerous lenity. If you are learned,
          Be not as common fools; if you are not,
          Then vail your ignorance. You are plebeians, &c. — In the

first of these lines, the original has *he* instead of *they*, and also the Roman type clauses in the second and fifth lines transposed. I adopt Hanmer's reading as the simplest and most satisfactory way of setting both the logic and the language in order. Collier's second folio substitutes *impotence* for *ignorance*, and thus gets a fitting antithesis to *power ;* but does nothing towards redressing the other difficulties of the passage. My own experience in proof-reading has taught me how apt lines and parts of lines are to get shuffled out of place in such cases. — In the second line, again, the original reads "*awake* your dangerous lenity"; which, it seems to me, cannot possibly be made to yield any consistent sense. *Revoke* is from Collier's second folio, which also substitutes *bounty* for *lenity*. The latter I can by no means accept; for Coriolanus is here speaking, not against the Senate's bounty in letting the people have corn *gratis*, but against their indulgent temper, or *lenity*, in letting them have Tribunes as their own special magistrates.

P. 111.   *Th' accusation*
    Which they have often made against the Senate,
    All cause unborn, could never be the motive
    Of our so frank donation. Well, what then ?
    How shall this bisson multitude *digest*
    The Senate's courtesy ? — In the third of these lines, the original has *Native* instead of *motive*, which was proposed by Heath. In the fifth line, also, the old text has *Bosome-multiplied* instead of *bisson multitude*, which is from Collier's second folio. It is indeed possible that *bosom multiplied* may have been intended as an equivalent for *multitudinous bosom*, which is a right Shakespearian expression. Still *multiplied* is but a flat and feeble substitute for *multitudinous*.

P. 112. Where one *part does disdain with cause, the other*
    Insult without all reason. — The original has *Whereon* instead of *Where one*. Rowe's correction.

P. 112. *To* jump *a body with a dangerous physic*
    That's sure of death without it. — Much question has been made of *jump* in this passage. Pope substituted *vamp*, which has been adopted by some editors. Singer reads *imp*, which is a term in falconry, signifying to graft or insert feathers into the damaged wing of a

hawk; and so running into a secondary meaning of to repair or re-store by artificial means.   To my surprise, Dyce adopts *imp*, and speaks of *jump* as a "rank corruption."   Staunton is confident we ought to read *purge ;* and, surely, this is much better than either *vamp* or *imp*. But I am quite satisfied with *jump*, which was often used in the sense of to *risk* or *hazard*.   The word occurs as a verb with that sense in the well-known speech of Macbeth, "We'd *jump* the life to come."   Like-wise as a substantive in *Antony and Cleopatra*, iii. 8: "Our fortune lies upon this *jump*."   The same use of the word is found in Hol-land's Pliny: "If we looke for good successe in our cure by ministring ellebore, &c., for certainly it putteth the patient to a *jumpe* or greate hazard."   Singer says of *jump* that "nothing can be made of it."   But, as explained by the above quotations, to *jump* a body is the very thing that would needs be done by using *dangerous physic ;* nor is any thing more natural or more common than to use such physic in cases where the patient is "sure of death without it."   In other words, the sense of *risk* agrees much better with the context here, than that of *mend*.

P. 114.   Sen. ⎫
         Pat. ⎬ *Weapons, weapons, weapons ! —*
         &c. ⎭
   Tribunes ! — Patricians ! — Citizens ! — What, ho ! —
   Sicinius ! — Brutus ! — Coriolanus ! — Citizens ! —
   Peace, peace, peace ! — Stay, hold, peace ! — To this speech the original prefixes merely "*2 Sen.*"   But it was clearly meant as a confused utterance of the assembled crowd, Senators, patricians, Tribunes, and others sharing in it.   The last line of the speech has "*All*" prefixed to it in the old text ; but it is evidently a part of the confused utterance which runs through the preceding lines : I there-fore concur with the Cambridge Editors and Dyce in throwing out the prefix.

P. 114.   *You, tribunes,*
     Speak *to the people ; — Coriolanus, patience ; —*
     Speak, good Sicinius. — The first *Speak*, which is plainly nec-essary to the sense, is wanting in the original.   The insertion is Tyr-whitt's.

P. 115. Cor. *That is the way to lay the city flat;* &c. — So Pope. The original prefixes " *Com.*" to this speech : but the following speech is conclusive that this rightly belongs to Coriolanus.

P. 115. *Be that you seem, truly your country's* friends, &c. — As this speech is certainly addressed to both the Tribunes, there can be no doubt that we ought to read *friends,* and not *friend,* as it is in the original. Corrected by Rowe.

P. 116. *Help,* help *Marcius, help,*
    You that be noble. — So Hanmer, Capell, and Walker. The original omits the second *help.*

P. 116. *Go, get you to* your *house; be gone, away !* — Instead of *your,* the original has *our,* which is palpably wrong. Rowe's correction.

P. 116. Cor.   *Stand fast;*
  We have as many friends as enemies. — Here, again, the original prefixes " *Com.*" Warburton clearly is right in saying that " this speech certainly should be given to Coriolanus ; for all his friends persuade him to retire."

P. 116. Com. *Come, sir, along with us.*
    Cor. *I would they were barbarians, as they are,*
   Though in Rome litter'd; not Romans, as they are not,
   Though calved i' the porch o' the Capitol, —
    Men.   *Be gone;*
  Put not your worthy rage into your tongue, &c. — So Tyrwhitt and Collier's second folio. The original runs the two latter speeches into one, and assigns the whole to Menenius. To the first speech, also, the original prefixes " *Corio.*" Corrected in the second folio.

P. 118.   *To eject him hence*
  Were but our *danger ; and to keep him here*
  Our certain death. — The original reads " Were but *one* danger." An obvious error, corrected by Theobald.

P. 119.   *The service of the foot,*
  Being once gangrened, is not then respected
  For what it was before. — Some **would** assign this speech **to**

Sicinius ; Lettsom would make it a part of Brutus' preceding speech, and then assign the next speech to Sicinius ; but I can hardly think the Poet would have put into the mouth of either Tribune an argument so palpably unjust.   See foot-note 31.

P. 120. *I'll go to him, and undertake to bring him*
           Where he shall answer, by a lawful form,—
           In peace,— to's utmost peril. — The original adds the words *in peace* to the first of these lines, — " bring him *in peace* " ; a repetition at odds alike with sense and metre.

ACT III., SCENE 2.

P. 122.   *Would you have me*
           False to my nature ?   Rather say, I play
           Truly the man I am. —So Hanmer. The original lacks *Truly*, which makes a fitting antithesis to *False* in the preceding line. Dr. Badham would read

>   False to my nature?   Rather say *you're glad*
>   I play the man I am.

P. 122.   *Lesser had been*
           The thwartings of your disposition, if
           You had not show'd them how you were disposed, &c. — The original reads "The *things* of your *dispositions*."   Theobald substituted *thwartings* for *things*.   Rowe printed "The things *that thwart*," &c. *Disposition* is Hanmer's reading.

P. 122. *I have a heart as* tickle-apt *as yours,*
           But yet a brain that leads my use of anger
           To better vantage. — The original reads " a heart as *little* apt," out of which it seems hardly possible to gather any fitting sense. For the present reading I am indebted to Mr. P. A. Daniel, of London. It seems to me to remove fairly the difficulty of the passage. See footnote 5, especially the quotation from Chapman. Collier's second folio endeavours in vain to mend the matter by interpolating a whole line thus :

> I have a heart as little apt as yours,
> *To brook control without the use of anger,*
> But yet a brain that leads my use of anger, &c.

P. 123. *Before he should thus stoop to th'* herd, &c. — So Theobald. The original has *heart* instead of *herd*.

P. 124.
> *Not by your own instruction,*
> *Nor by the matter which your* own *heart prompts you,*
> *But with such words that are but* roted *in*
> *Your tongue,* thought's *bastards, and* but *syllables*
> *Of no* allowance *to your bosom's truth.* — So Dr. Badham, in *Cambridge Essays,* 1856. The original lacks *own* in the second line, and in the third reads "*though but* Bastards, and Syllables." This is manifestly neither metre nor logic ; and I think the correction sets the line in excellent order in both these respects. Of course "thought's bastards" means the *spurious,* not the *legitimate offspring* of the mind. — In the second line, the original has "that are but *roated* in." It may be something doubtful what *roated* was meant for ; and some editors change it to *rooted;* but I think *roted* gives a more congruent sense, and is equally good English. Of course it means *spoken by rote.* — In the last line, again, Johnson proposed, and Capell printed, *alliance* instead of *allowance.* I was once led to favour *alliance,* but am now thoroughly satisfied that *allowance* is right. See foot-note 7.

P. 125. *Go to them, with this bonnet in thy hand;*
> *And — thus far having stretch'd it, waving thy head,*
> *Which often, thus, correcting thy stout heart,*
> Bow, *humble as the ripest mulberry*
> *That will not hold the handling, — say to them,* &c. — In the fourth of these lines, the original has *Now* instead of *Bow,* thus leaving *Which* without any syntactical connection. The correction is Mason's. — In the last line, again, the original has "*or* say," against both sense and metre. Corrected by Hanmer, who is followed by White and Dyce.

P. 125.
> *This but done,*
> *Even as she speaks* it, *why, their hearts were yours.* — So Capell and Ritson. The original lacks *it.*

P. 126. *Must I go show them my unbarbèd sconce?*
          Must I with my base tongue give to my heart
              A lie that it must bear? — The original reads "to my *noble*
heart"; where *noble* is redundant in metre, and worse than redundant
in sense: it fairly contradicts the hero's proper tone. An interpolation,
I have no doubt.

P. 127.   *Into a pipe*
          Small as an eunuch's, *or the virgin voice*
              That babies lulls *asleep.* — The original has *Eunuch* and *lull.*
Hardly worth noting, perhaps.

P. 128. *Thy valiantness was mine, thou suck'dst it from me,*
              But owest *thy pride thyself.* — So Collier's second folio. The
original has *owe.*

ACT III., SCENE 3.

P. 129. *I have; 'tis ready* here. — The word *here* is not in the original, but seems fairly warranted on grounds both of metre and of sense.
Supplied by Pope.

P. 130.   *He hath been used*
          Ever to conquer, and to have his word
              Of contradiction. — So Rowe. Instead of *word*, the original
has *worth*, which seems to me absolutely meaningless here. On the
other hand, *word* seems rather tame for the occasion. Collier's second
folio has *mouth*, which is dreadful. Lettsom suggests *will*, which is far
from happy, *me judice.* Becket conjectures *wroth;* and thereupon
Mr. P. A. Daniel proposes a reading which, though something bold,
seems to me well worth considering, "and to *heat* his *wrath On* contradiction."

P. 130. Throng *our large temples with the shows of peace.* — The
original has *Through* instead of *Throng.* Corrected by Theobald.

P. 131.   *Do not take*
          His rougher accents *for malicious sounds.* — The original has
Actions for *accents.* Corrected by Theobald.

P. 133. *Nor check my* courage *for what they can give.* — For *courage* Collier's second folio substitutes *carriage*, which seems to me not unlikely to be the true reading.

P. 133. *For that he has,*
As much as in him lies, from time to time,
Inveigh'd *against the people, seeking means*
To pluck away their power ; &c. — The original has "*Envied* against." It appears that *inveigh'd* was sometimes spelt *invaied*, which might easily be mistaken for *envied*. Dr. Badham observes that " to *envy against* a person or thing is foreign to the language, and there was nothing to induce Shakespeare to adopt such a construction." He also quotes from Lyly's *Euphues* a passage where the author plays upon the resemblance of the two words : " Although I have been bolde to *invay* against many, yet I am not so brutish as to envy them all." The reading in the text was proposed by Becket.

P. 133. *I have been Consul, and can show* for *Rome*
Her enemies' marks upon me. — The original has *from* instead of *for*. Corrected by Theobald.

P. 134. *Making* but *reservation of yourselves.* — Capell and Collier's second folio substitute *not* for *but ;* and Dyce follows them. The change appears to me something worse than unnecessary, since it would imply that the people *banished themselves*, after having banished their defenders. See foot-note 9.

P. 135. *Despising,* then,
For you, the city, thus I turn my back. — The original lacks *then*. Some such word is clearly needed both for logic and metre. Inserted by Pope.

P. 135. *Come, come, let's see him out at gates ; come,* come ; —
The gods preserve our noble tribunes ! — come. — The last *come* in the first of these lines is wanting in the original.

ACT IV., SCENE 1.

P. 136. *You were used*
To say extremity *was the trier of spirits.* — So the second folio. The first has " *Extreamities* was," &c.

P. 136.   *Fortune's blows*
    When most struck home, being gentle-minded *craves*
    A noble cunning. — So Collier's second folio.   The original has
" being *gentle wounded*," upon which editors have exercised their wits
somewhat variously in correction.   Pope reads " being gently *warded*,"
Hanmer, " being *greatly warded*."   See foot-note 1.

P. 137.   *My* fair *son,*
    Whither wilt thou go?   Take good Cominius, &c. — The
original has " My *first* son," with which all are dissatisfied, I believe, as
indeed they may well be.   Heath proposed " My *fierce* son," and Hanmer printed " *First, my* son," neither of which is any improvement.
Shakespeare uses *fair* in a great variety of senses, among which those
of *brave, noble, high-minded* are repeatedly included.

Act iv., Scene 2.

P. 139.   *O, ye're well met : the hoarded* plagues *o' the gods*
    Requite your loves! — The original has *plague* instead of *plagues.*
The correction was proposed by Lettsom, and is right, surely.   See
foot-note 1.

P. 139.   *More noble blows than ever thou* wise *words;*
    And for Rome's good. — Lettsom would read " thou *vile* words ";
and he observes that " at any rate *wise* is preposterous."   The word
does not indeed seem just right ; but I cannot see that *vile* does much
better.   I suspect we ought to read " *mere* words."

P. 139.   Vol.   *What then!*
    He'd make an end of thy posterity,
    Bastards and all.   Good man, the wounds that he
    Does bear for Rome! — So Hanmer.   The original gives the
first part of the speech, all before *Good*, to Virgilia.   It seems quite out
of keeping with her character ; while the whole is in perfect keeping
with that of Volumnia.

Act IV., Scene 3.

P. 141. *You had more beard when I last saw you ; but your favour is well* appear'd *by your tongue.* — This use of *appear'd* seems rather strange to us. Steevens conjectured *approved*, which is substituted in Collier's second folio ; and so Dyce prints. Various other substitutes have been adopted or proposed ; the most noteworthy of which is *appayed*, given by Singer on the ground of its being an old word for " *satisfied, contented* " *! !* It is evident that the authors of these changes did not understand the Poet's use of to *appear*. Mr. Joseph Crosby has satisfied me in the matter by pointing out a good many instances where that word is clearly used as a transitive verb, meaning to *show*, to *manifest*, to *make apparent*, to *present*, &c. So in *Troilus and Cressida*, iii. 3 : " *Appear* it to your mind that, through the sight I bear in things to come." See, also, page 98, note 10, and *Cymbeline*, page 138, note 8.

Act IV., Scene 4.

P. 143. *Whose* house, *whose bed, whose meal, and exercise,*
  Are still together, &c. — So Collier's second folio, and rightly, beyond all question. The original has *Houres* instead of *house*.

P. 144. *My birth-place* hate I, *and my love's upon*
  This enemy's *town.* — The original reads " My Birth-place *have* I." Corrected by Capell. The original also has " This *Enemie* Towne." As the word was probably written *Enemies*, the misprint was easy. The correction was made in the fourth folio, and is fully justified by the words just after, " if *he* slay me."

Act IV., Scene 5.

P. 144. *Has the porter* no *eyes in his head, that he gives entrance to such companions ?* — The original has *his* instead of *no ;* doubtless an accidental repetition from the words immediately following.

P. 146.   *If, Tullus,*
  Not yet thou knowest me, and, seeing me, dost not
  Think me the man I am, necessity

Commands me name myself. — The original reads " thinke me
for the man," &c.   Capell struck out *for ;* and Lettsom is surely right
in saying that the expression *think for* is not English.

P. 148.   *If Jupiter*
      Should from out yonder *cloud speak divine things,*
      And say 'Tis true, I'd not believe him *more*
      Than thee, all-noble Marcius. — The original has the second of
these lines thus : " Should from *yond* clowd speake divine things."   It
is hardly credible that the Poet should here have written such a muti-
lated verse.   Pope printed " Should from yon cloud speak *to me things
divine.*"   The reading in the text was proposed by Dyce. — In the third
line, also, the old text has *them* instead of *him,* which is Walker's correction.

P. 148.   *And* scarr'd *the Moon with splinters.* — The original prints
scarr'd, which Collier's second folio alters to *scar'd.*   As the two words
scarr'd and *scared* were often spelt alike, it is something doubtful
which of them the Poet intended here.   See foot-note 8.

P. 149.   *Had we no quarrel else to Rome, but that*
      Thou art thence banish'd, &c. — So the third folio.   The earlier
editions read " Had we no *other* quarrell else."

P. 149.   *To fright them, ere destroy.   But come* thou *in :*
      Let me commend thee first, &c. — The original reads " But
come in."   As there ought, evidently, to be no halting in the metre
here, the usual reading has been " But come, *come* in."   Lettsom proposed " But *now* come in."   It seems to me that *thou* is the simplest
way of completing the verse.

P. 150.   *But a greater soldier than he you wot* on. — The original
has " you wot *one.*"   Dyce's correction.

P. 151.   *An he had been cannibally given, he might have* broil'd *and
eaten him too.* — The original has *boyld* instead of *broil'd.*   Corrected
by Pope.

P. 152.   *This peace is nothing but to rust iron,* &c. — Capell reads
" This peace is *good for* nothing," &c.   Rightly, I suspect.   Some have
printed " is *worth* nothing."

P. 152. *It's sprightly,* waking, *audible, and full of vent.* — The original has *walking,* instead of *waking.* Pope's correction.

P. 152. *Peace is a very apoplexy,* a *lethargy ;* mute, *deaf,* sleepy, *insensible ;* &c. — So Walker. The old text lacks *a* before *lethargy,* and has *mull'd* instead of *mute.* The common explanation of *mull'd* is "softened and dispirited, as wine is when burnt and sweetened." But what has that sense to do along with *deaf?* The third folio has *sleepy,* the older text being *sleepe.*

ACT IV., SCENE 6.

P. 153. *We hear not of him, neither need we fear him ;*
 His remedies are tame : the present peace
 And quietness of the people, which before
 Were in wild hurry, here do make his friends
 Blush that the world goes well ; &c. — Here I am induced, by clear reasons both of logic and of metre, to adopt the reading of Hanmer. In the original the passage is printed thus :

> We heare not of him, neither need we fear him,
> His remedies are tame, the present peace,
> And quietnesse of the people, which before
> Were in wilde hurry. Heere do we make his Friends
> Blush, that the world goes well.

Some change is evidently required in order to make any sense at all of the passage : and Theobald's change, which some adopt, " His remedies are tame *i' the* present peace," &c., saves neither the metre nor the logic. In the fourth line, *we* is palpably redundant in verse and paralogical in sense ; the speaker's drift being, not that *we,* the Tribunes, but that the continued peace and quietness of the people, make the patricians ashamed of having predicted popular commotions as the consequence of the hero's banishment.

P. 153. *Bru.*   •   Hail, sir !
   Men.   *Hail to you both !*
   Sic. *Your Coriolanus,* sir, *is not much miss'd*
   But with his friends. — The words, *Hail, sir !* together with the prefix " *Bru.*", are wanting in the original, doubtless by accidental

omission, as both the metre and the reply of Menenius require them.
Supplied by Capell. — In the speech of Sicinius, also, *sir*, wanting in
the old text, was inserted by Capell.

P. 154. *Ourselves, our wives, and children, on our knees,*
　　　　Are bound to pray for both you. — The original reads "to pray
for *you both.*"

P. 155. 　　　　　*And affecting one sole throne,*
　　　　Without assistance.
　　　　　Men. 　　　　　　　Nay, *I think not so.* — The original lacks
Nay, thus leaving a gap in the verse, which Walker thought it so im-
portant to have filled, that he proposed to read *assistancy.* Pope inserted
Nay.

P. 155. *We should by this, to all our lamentation,*
　　　　If he had gone forth Consul, so have *found it.* — The original
reads "found it *so*"; thus giving us the construction, "*should found*
it so," which is not English, and, I think, never was.

P. 156. *The nobles in great earnestness are going*
　　　　All to the Senate-house : some news is come
　　　　That turns their countenances. — The original has *comming*
instead of *come ;* doubtless an accidental repetition from the ending of
the line before. Rowe's correction.

P. 156. *He and Aufidius can no more atone*
　　　　Than violentest contrarieties. — So Hanmer. The original has
Contrariety.

P. 158. *Are mock'd for valiant ignorance.* — I suspect we ought to
read, with Hanmer, "Are *only* mock'd."

ACT IV., SCENE 7.　　•

P. 163. 　　　　　　　*So our* virtues
　　　　Lie in th' interpretation of the time. — So the second folio.
The original has " *Vertue* Lie." Collier's second folio substitutes *Live*

for *Lie*. Mr. A. E. Brae is for reading "So *doth* virtue Lie"; and I am apt to think that the right text.

P. 163. *And power, unto itself most cômmendable,*
    Hath not a tomb so evident as a chair,
      T' extol what it hath done. — This passage has been a prodigious puzzle to the editors, most of whom have thought it badly corrupted. Various changes have been made or proposed, some in *evident*, but more in *chair ;* such as *cheer*, in Collier's second folio ; *hair*, by Singer; *claim*, by Leo ; *care*, by Mitford ; and *tear*, by myself. White has conjectured the true reading to be "Hath not a *tongue* so *eloquent* as a chair." I am now thoroughly satisfied that the old text is right ; or that, if any change is wanted, it should be "Hath *ne'er* a tomb." And I am indebted for this, in the first instance, to Mr. Joseph Crosby ; though I since find that Staunton and Mr. R. Whitelaw have given substantially the same solution of the difficulty. The changes made and proposed have all proceeded upon the supposal that the construction is, "Hath not a tomb to extol"; whereas the construction is, "a chair to extol," that is, "a chair *that extols*." With this key to the meaning, the old text is readily seen to be right. See foot-notes 7 and 8.

P. 164. *Rights by rights fouler, strengths by strengths, do fail.* — Here, again, the text has been generally held corrupt, and divers changes have been made or proposed ; such as, "*Right's* by *right foulèd*," "*Right's* by *right* failèd," "Rights by rights *foul are*," "Rights by rights *founder*," "Rights by rights *suffer*," "Rights by rights *fail'd are*," and "Rights by rights *falter*." Dyce observes, "That a verb lies concealed under the corruption *fouler* is indubitable." But this is now far from being indubitable to me : I believe the old text to be right. See foot-note 10.

ACT V., SCENE I.

P. 165. *A pair of tribunes that have wreck'd* fair *Rome*
    To make coals cheap, — A noble memory ! — The original reads "have *wrack'd for* Rome." Hanmer changed this to "have *sack'd fair* Rome." Others have turned *wrack'd* into *rack'd*. The reading

in the text was proposed by Mr. W. W. Williams in *The Parthenon* for May 3, 1862 ; with the observation, "We meet elsewhere in Shakespeare with 'fair Athens,' 'fair Milan,' and 'fair Verona': and why not *fair Rome*, — that 'urbs pulcherrima'?"

P. 165. *I minded him how royal 'twas to pardon*
     When it was least *expected : he replied,*
     It was a rare *petition of a State*
     To one whom they had punish'd. — In the second of these lines, the original has *lesse* instead of *least;* also, in the third, *bare* instead of *rare.* The latter correction was proposed by Mr. W. W. Williams in *The Parthenon*, May 3, 1862 ; who quotes from i. 1 : "And *a petition* granted them, a *strange* one." The meaning of *rare* in this instance is *strange* or *extraordinary.* Singer thinks we should read "a *base* petition." The correction of lesse to *least* is Pope's.

P. 165. *He could not stay to pick them in a pile*
     Of noisome musty chaff : he said 'twas folly,
     For one poor grain or two, to leave't *unburnt,*
     And still to nose th' offence. — The old text reads "to *leave* unburnt." The slight addition, *'t,* is proposed by Mr. P. A. Daniel, who fitly. observes, "you may 'nose' an offence ; but can only burn that which produces it." Of course "leave*t* unburnt" refers to the pile of chaff.

P. 166. *Pray you* now, *go to him.* So Dyce. The original lacks *now.* The insertion, besides being wanted for the metre, is sustained from iii. 2 : "I pr'ythee *now,* my son, go to them," &c.

P. 166.   *Well, and say that Marcius*
     Return me, as Cominus is return'd,
     Unheard ; what then? or not unheard, *but as*
     A discontented friend, grief-shot with his
     Unkindness?
     Sic,   Say't be so, *yet your good will*
     Must have that thanks from Rome, &c. — The original has this passage badly mutilated and disordered : the words *or not unheard* are there wanting altogether ; and the words *Say't be so* are made to close

the preceding speech. Both Hanmer and Capell tried their hands at amendment, but without much success. Dr. Badham does better; whose reading I have adopted.

P. 167. *Speed how it will*, you *shall ere long have knowledge*
   Of my success. — So Heath and Collier's second folio. The original has *I* instead of *you;* doubtless an accidental repetition from the preceding line. The old reading comes pretty near being absurd; as Menenius could not well remain ignorant of his own success.

P. 167.   *What he would do,*
   He sent in writing after me, what he would not;
   Bound with an oath to yield to his conditions. — This passage is very troublesome: as commonly pointed, it is quite unintelligible, if not unmeaning. Very likely it is corrupt; but, if so, it is not easy to fix upon the precise point where. Staunton proposes to read "Bound with an oath to yield to *no* conditions." Leo says, " Professor Solly suggested to me, as a new reading, *hold* for *yield*." I more than suspect this latter to be the true reading. See foot-note 9.

P. 167. *So that all hope is vain,*
   Unless in's *noble mother and his wife;*
   Who, as I hear, mean to solicit him, &c. — The original reads " Unless *his* Noble Mother," &c. The reading in the text was suggested to Steevens. Of course *unless* is here equivalent to *except;* and such contractions as *in's* for *in his* are frequent in the Poet's later plays.

ACT V., SCENE 2.

P. 168.   *I have been*
   The book of his good acts, whence men have read
   His fame unparallel'd, haply amplified;
   For I have ever amplified *my friends*, &c. — Instead of the second *amplified*, the original has *verified*, which probably crept in from *verity* in the next line. Hanmer and Collier's second folio substitute *magnified*. Lettsom asks, " Why not repeat *amplified?*" Surely it is much better so.

P. 169. *Think to front his revenges with the* easy *groans of old women*, &c. — For *easy* Collier's second folio substitutes *queasy*, and Staunton proposes *wheezy*. But *easy* may well bear a sense not unfitting, — *slight, cheap, not worth minding.*

P. 170. *Guess, but* by *my entertainment with him, if thou stand'st not i' the state of hanging*, &c. — So Malone. The word *by*, necessary to the sense, is wanting in the original.

P. 170. *I have been blown out of* our *gates with sighs*. — So the fourth folio. The earlier editions have *your* instead of *our*.

ACT V., SCENE 3.

P. 174.　　　　　　　　　　*You gods ! I prate,*
　　　And the most noble mother of the world
　　　Leave unsaluted. — So Theobald. The original has *pray* instead of *prate*.

P. 174. *Then let the pebbles on the* angry *beach*
　　　Fillip the stars ; &c. — The original reads "the *hungry* beach," which has been variously explained as "the sterile, unprolific beach," and as "the beach hungry or eager for shipwrecks, *littus avarum*." So that, as an epithet of *beach*, taken by itself, *hungry* may well pass ; but that sense has no coherence with the context here. Malone conjectured *angry*.

P. 175. *The* things *I have forsworn to grant may never*
　　　Be held by you denials. — The original has *thing*. The word *denials* shows that it should be *things*.

P. 176.　　　　　　　　　　*Yet we'll ask ;*
　　　That, if we fail in our *request, the blame*
　　　May hang upon your hardness. — The original reads "if we fail in *your* request"; *your* having doubtless been accidentally repeated from the line below. Rowe's correction.

P. 177.　　　　　　　　　　*Thou shalt no sooner*
　　　March to assault thy country than to tread —
　　　Trust to't thou shalt not — on thy mother's womb,

> *That brought thee to this world.*
>
> Vir.   *Ay, and on mine,*
>
> *That brought you forth this boy*, &c. — The original has merely "I, and mine." Capell inserted *on*. That the omission was accidental, who can doubt?

P. 177.   *'A shall not tread on me:*

I'll run away till I am bigger, then I'll fight. — The old text reads "till I am bigger, *but* then Ile fight." Here *but* manifestly spoils the metre without helping the sense.

P. 178. *Thou hast affected the* fine *strains of honour.* — The original has *five* instead of *fine*. Corrected by Johnson.

P. 178. *And yet to* charge *thy sulphur with a bolt*, &c. — The original has *change* instead of *charge*. The same misprint has occurred before in this play. See note on "From whom I have received not only greetings," &c., page 198.

P. 179. *Down, ladies; let us shame him with our knees.* — So the second folio. The first reads "let us shame him with *him* our knees." Not worth noting, perhaps

P. 179. *This fellow had a Volscian to his mother;*

> *His wife is in Corioli, and* this *child*

Like him by chance. — The original has "and *his* child." The correction is Theobald's, who notes as follows: "Volumnia would hint that Coriolanus by his stern behaviour had lost all family regards, and did not remember that he had any child. 'I am not his mother,' says she; 'his wife is in Corioli; and *this* child, whom we bring with us, is not his child, but only bears his resemblance by chance.'"

P. 179.   *Now, good Aufidius,*

> *Were you in my stead*, say, *would you have heard*

A mother less? — So Pope. The original lacks *say*, thus leaving a gap in the verse where it is plain there ought to be none.

P. 180.   *Out of that I'll work*

    Myself a firmer *fortune.* — So Collier's second folio. The original has "a *former* Fortune."

P. 180.   *We will* but *drink together; and you shall bear*

    A better witness back than words, &c. — The original reads "*But* we will drink," &c. This naturally implies that the speaker purposes to join the ladies in a drink of wine. White observes, as he well may, "I cannot but believe that *drink,* addressed to Volumnia and Virgilia, is a corruption." See foot-note 12.

ACT V., SCENE 4.

P. 182.   *Art certain this is true ?*

    2 Mess.   Ay, sir, *most certain,* —

    As certain as I know the Sun is fire : &c. — I here adopt, without any misgiving, the reading and arrangement proposed by Lettsom. The original gives the passage thus :

        Art *thou* certaine this is true ? *Is't* most certaine.
        Mess. As certaine as I know the Sun is fire.

In the first line, Pope omitted *thou;* and modern editions set an (?) after "most certain." Referring to the phrases, "Art thou certain ?" and "Is it certain ?" Lettsom remarks as follows : "Shakespeare could scarcely have jumbled the phrases together so awkwardly as he appears from the editions to have done. *Is't* (as the old copies print it) is a misprint for *I sir,* that is, *Ay, sir,* and here the Messenger begins his answer to Sicinius." This is said in one of his notes on Walker, *Shakespeare's Versification,* page 285. Afterwards, in a letter to Dyce, he adds the following : "It is not at all likely, or rather it is quite impossible, that a person would begin with '*Art* THOU certain this is true ?' and then go on, '*is* IT most certain ?' He would say, '*art thou* most certain ?'"

ACT V., SCENE 6.

P. 183.   "SCENE VI. — Corioli." — This scene, the place of which is not told in the old copies, used to be marked at "*Antium,*" till Singer substituted "*Corioli.*"

P. 184. *He bow'd his nature, never known before*
　　　But to be rough, unswayable, and fierce. — So Hanmer and Collier's second folio. The original has *free* instead of *fierce*.

P. 185.　　　　　　　　　*Holp to* reap *the fame*
　　　Which he did end *all his.* — This has commonly been thought corrupt, and various changes have been made or proposed. Rowe substituted *make* for *end*. Some would substitute *ear* for *reap*, and *reap* for *end;* others would substitute *bind* for *end*. But the old text has been amply vindicated by the Rev. Mr. Arrowsmith. See foot-note 1.

P. 188. *That pages blush'd at him, and men of heart*
　　　Look'd wondering each at other. — The original reads "each a *others*." Corrected by Rowe.

P. 188. *That, like an eagle in a dove-cote, I*
　　　Flutter'd *your Volscians in Corioli*. The original has *Flatter'd,* instead of *Flutter'd*. Corrected in the third folio.

BOOKS IN HIGHER ENGLISH

Alexander's Introduction to Browning $1.00

Athenæum Press Series : 16 volumes of this Series are now ready. Other volumes are in preparation. See circulars for details.

Baker's Principles of Argumentation 1.12

Cook's First Book in Old English 1.50

Cook's Shelley's Defense of Poetry .... .50

Cook's Art of Poetry 1.12

Cook's Hunt's " What is Poetry ?" .... .50

Cook's Addison's Criticisms on Paradise Lost 1.00

Corson's Primer of English Verse 1.00

Emery's Notes on English Literature 1.00

Frink's New Century Speaker 1.00

Fulton and Trueblood's Practical Elocution 1.50

Fulton and Trueblood's Choice Readings 1.50

Garnett's English Prose from Elizabeth to Victoria 1.50

Gayley's Classic Myths in English Literature 1.50

Gummere's Handbook of Poetics 1.00

Holyoake's Public Speaking and Debate 1.00

Hudson's Harvard Edition of Shakespeare's Complete Works....

Hudson's Life, Art, and Characters of Shakespeare. 2 vols......... 4.00

Hudson's New School Shakespeare. Each play : paper, .30 ; cloth .45

Hudson's Text-Book of Poetry 1.25

Hudson's Text-Book of Prose 1.25

Hudson's Classical English Reader 1.00

Kent's Shakespeare Note-Book .... .60

Litchfield's Spenser's Britomart .... .60

Maxcy's Tragedy of Hamlet .... .45

Minto's Manual of English Prose Literature 1.50

Minto's Characteristics of English Poets 1.50

Phelps' English Romantic Movement 1.00

Sherman's Analytics of Literature 1.25

Smith's Synopsis of English and American Literature .... .80

Standard English Classics : 13 volumes of this Series are now ready. Other volumes are in preparation. See circulars for details.

Thayer's Best Elizabethan Plays 1.25

White's Philosophy of American Literature .... .30

White's Philosophy of English Literature 1.00

Winchester's Five Short Courses of Reading in English Literature .40

GINN & COMPANY, Publishers,

Boston.   New York.   Chicago.   Atlanta.   Dallas.

BOOKS ON ENGLISH LITERATURE

GINN & COMPANY, Publishers,

Boston.   New York.   Chicago.   Atlanta.   Dallas.